By Andrei Codrescu

Poetry

Alien Candor: Selected Poems 1970–1995 (1996)
Belligerence (1991)
Comrade Past & Mister Present (1987, 1991)
Selected Poems: 1970–1980 (1983)
Diapers on the Snow (1981)
Necrocorrida (1980)
For the Love of a Coat (1978)
The Lady Painter (1977)
The Marriage of Insult & Injury (1977)
A Mote Suite for Jan & Anselm (1976)
Grammar & Money (1973)
A Serious Morning (1973)
Secret Training (1973)
the, here, what, where (1972)
The History of the Growth of Heaven (1971, 1973)
License to Carry a Gun (1970)

Fiction

The Blood Countess (1995, 1996)
Monsieur Teste in America & Other Instances of Realism (1987)
The Repentance of Lorraine (1976, 1993)
Why I Can't Talk on the Telephone (1971)

Memoirs

Road Scholar: Coast to Coast Late in the Century. Photographs by
     David Graham. (1993)
The Hole in the Flag: an Exile's Story of Return & Revolution (1991)
In America's Shoes (1983)
The Life & Times of an Involuntary Genius (1975)

Essays

The Dog with the Chip in His Neck (1996)
Zombification (1994, 1995)
The Muse Is Always Half-Dressed in New Orleans (1993, 1995)
The Disappearance of the Outside (1990)
Raised by Puppets Only to be Killed by Research (1989)
A Craving for Swan (1986, 1987)

Translation

At the Court of Yearning: the Poems of Lucian Blaga (1989)
For Max Jacob (1974)

ANDREI CODRESCU

ALIEN CANDOR

SELECTED POEMS 1970–1995

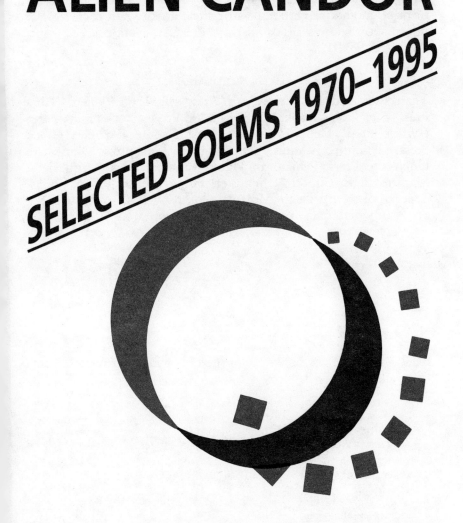

BLACK SPARROW PRESS ▪ SANTA ROSA ▪ 1996

ACKNOWLEDGMENTS

Thanks to: Addison-Wesley, Arif Press, Big Table/Follett, Capra Press, City Lights Books, Coffee House Press, Crow's Foot Press, Cymric Press, Dell, The Four Zoas, George Braziller, Grape Press, Hyperion, Isthmus Press, kingdom kum press, Ohio State University Press, Panjandrum Press, Picador, Pocket Books, St. Martin's Press, Simon & Schuster, Stone Post Art, Sun Books, Tree Books & William Morrow Company who published the books in which many of these poems first appeared.

LIBRARY OF CONGRESS CATALOGING-IN-PUBLICATION DATA

Codrescu, Andrei, 1946–
    Alien candor : selected poems, 1970–1995 / Andrei Codrescu.
    p. cm.
    ISBN 1-57423-013-1 (pbk. : alk. paper). — ISBN 1-57423-014-X
(cloth trade : alk. paper). — ISBN 1-57423-015-8 (signed cloth : alk. paper)
    I. Title.
. PS3553.03A79   1996
    811'.54.—dc20
                                       96-28360
                                     CIP

TABLE OF CONTENTS

SAN FRANCISCO (1973–1974)

MONTE RIO (1974–1978)

BALTIMORE (1980–1981)

BATON ROUGE & NEW ORLEANS (1986–1995)

Retrospection is an anguished operation, involving as it does, a territorial perspective, as well as a claim to poetic identity. The territory is fairly well drawn. Where it overlaps with the regions of others, the areas are joyously recognized and credit is amply given. As for the latter, the effort was simply, as Ted Berrigan put it in "People of the Future": "people of the future / when you are reading these poems / remember / you didn't write them / I did." These are poems written in English by one who learned the language as he wrote them. The earliest, "personae" poems, in "License to Carry a Gun" and "The History of the Growth of Heaven" are Romanian poems with an American mask on. To paraphrase Virgil Gheorghiu, another language-jumper: I wrote them in Romanian but I expressed myself in English.

I began learning American in 1966 when I came to America. I had written in Romanian for at least four years and I was convinced of my vocation. Language did not seem all that important. As a New York poet once put it: I use language the way I use public transportation. The main thing was being a poet. As soon as I had three to four words in my new language, I started linking them and writing them down, mostly on girls' arms. I was 19 and I had urgent things to tell them. The mid-sixties on the Lower East Side of New York were a blessed time. It was Paris in the twenties, Bucharest in the teens, only better, because there was a whole poetic generation to test the enterprise. America was 19 years old and so was I. My poetic exile happened to correspond with the metaphorical exile of a whole generation. In Eastern Europe poets had been valued because they carried the weight of a complete opposition. In America, without missing a beat, the job was the same. For many blessed reasons, we were suddenly free, east and west. It was freedom wrenched from a poetic rejection of prevailing values. New York being New York, however, the irony of any "revolutionary" enterprise was present at all times. I was lucky to meet, in 1968, Ted Berrigan, Anne Waldman, Lewis Warsh, Michael Stephens, Paul Blackburn, Joel Oppenheimer. These were true Americans, solidly middle-class bohemians who practiced the American language sturdily, with a passion for the new but a keen sense of the ridiculous, which surrounded us at every turn. Nothing shocked my Romanian metaphysical sensibilities more than Ted Berrigan's absolutely insistent attention to the seemingly trivial. Of course, this wasn't the case, as it became apparent on further reading: he was employing "non-poetic" language because, amazingly, few American poets had. Steeped as I was in the sacerdotal surrealism of Lucian Blaga, my main childhood influence, I felt as if I discovered the world at last. My compatriot, Tristan Tzara, had, of course, discovered that world first and Ted was treading, brilliantly, on his grounds. And those of the Beats, whose Dada-Rimbaudian-Barnum & Baileyesque performance was as much part of the air as Bob Dylan's incomprehensible lyrics. (Meaning, I couldn't understand a word he said, and so I wrote down what I *thought* he said, creating in the process a whole Dylan oeuvre by *me*.)

My luck and my education held to the end of the decade (which closed, properly, in 1973) because I developed solid friendships with the poets I admired. I worked for a time at the Eighth Street Bookshop, the greatest bookstore on earth, where New York writers shopped and gossiped. What they read, we read. We didn't miss anything. If Edward Albee came in and bought an obscure military history we had that read, discussed and questioned by the end of the next working day. The intoxicating privilege of being a young poet at the center of things carried me through the transition to English, a painful process vouchsafed to few immigrants before or after. In addition, mimeographed journals like "The World," edited by Anne Waldman and Lewis Warsh as the St. Marks' poetry project, published my poems as fast as I could write them. Poetry, my poetry, was news. In 1970, I moved to San Francisco, where the era of the Poetry Reading began. The explosion of verse performance demanded a yet more public tone and a collaborative approach. I wrote poetry with Tom Veitch, Terry Patten, Michael Palmer, Aram Saroyan, Lewis MacAdams, Kit Robinson, Jim Gustafson, Pat Nolan and many others. I also wrote quickly on napkins at Vesuvio's in order to have something to read at the Coffee Gallery for the free beer and wine. I edited mimeograph books (kingdom kum press) and magazines and helped found the Intersection Poetry series. All this activity, coupled with the benign tolerance of San Francisco, and the constant promise of pleasure in the air, gave my poems an exalted and happy feeling that still makes me giddy.

In 1974, Alice and I and our son Lucian, moved to Monte Rio, a small town in the redwoods of Northern California. We were dirt poor, as was everyone around us, but the communal bonds and close friendships made everything OK. My good friend Pat Nolan lived here and soon a wonderful young poet, Jeffrey

Miller, moved in. I described this scene in my autobiographical book, *In America's Shoes*, and I wish to add only that it was a time of darkening and deepening for my writing. I started attempting to free-lance prose too at this time, hoping to make some money. When Jeffrey died in a car accident in 1977, a distinct closure came to my writing as well.

The years from 1977 until 1984 were spent in Baltimore where the job of making a living took some serious consideration. My son Tristan was born. I began writing an opinion column for the *Baltimore Sun*. I started teaching literature at Johns Hopkins University. I began writing radio essays for NPR. And I founded *Exquisite Corpse*, a journal of poetry and essays that continues in good health to this day. My poetry now took on a sober rage, as I see it, filled with the details of an argument about the freedom of poetry (for it!) that still preoccupies me.

In 1984, I was hired to teach at Louisiana State University in Baton Rouge and we left the East Coast, completing a migration that, Hopi-style, went East to West, West to East, and East to South. Which leaves only North still. The South was a return to roots, somehow, because here I found the love of living and tropical indolence of the Balkans, combined with the love for living language that was sucked out of most places by television and urban discomfort. Poems of this period are more capacious and unafraid, I hope, to take on matter that earlier works were too skittish to accommodate. I also wrote longer poems that are not merely a display of lyric fragments. In 1988, the red-fascist dictatorship of Nicolae Ceausescu collapsed in Romania. I returned, for the first time in a quarter of a century, to cover the events for NPR and ABC News. Another period of my life and work was neatly bracketed. The Romanian poets I had admired were thrown into disarray by the suicide of Communism. They now look to the West for some hint of how to survive within the loosed waters of reportage and kitsch. I feel for them and hope that some of these poems contain clues.

All this biographical material explains *something*. What I left out is the polemical defense of the territory. The last twenty years in American poetry have been the site of an epic battleground for competing claims about what poetry is, does, should do, can do. An anthology I edited, *American Poets Since 1970: Up Late*, takes up arms on behalf of certain poetries, namely New York School, East Coast Zen & Surrealism, and Performance poetry. As such, this is a moment in time marked, on the left, by Language poetry

and on the right by the return of so-called academic "formalism."
I am only bringing this up here to note that my own work has
had its own lyric momentum and mysterious drive that has little
to do with the quarrels in question. And there is no small
perversity involved: the work often displays what I have attacked
in others and attacks what I profess to love. I don't want to do the
critic's job here but, gee, if we only *had* critics. "Our mistake,"
Ted used to say, "is that we didn't raise our own critics." I've
been quoting that to no avail to my academic colleagues. They
still prefer the dead. And speaking of the dead, I offer this
collection to mine: Ted Berrigan, Jeffrey Miller, Joe Cardarelli,
E.M. Cioran, Mircea Eliade, Ioan Coulianou, Gherasim Luca,
Paul Blackburn, and Joel Oppenheimer. I hope they dig it.

Andrei Codrescu
New Orleans, January 14, 1996

ALIEN CANDOR

SELECTED POEMS 1970–1995

Personae: Sibiu to New York
1970–1972

The poems in this section are the work of four imaginary poets: Julio Hernandez, Peter Boone, Alice Henderson-Codrescu, and Calvin Boone. Each of them was meant to have a career and a biography, independent of myself. I imagined them taking off, like Fernando Pessoa's "heteronyms," into public life. Circumstances didn't allow them an independent publishing career. Julio, Peter, and Alice ended up under the single cover of a book called *License to Carry a Gun* by Andrei Codrescu, while Calvin Boone became the central figure of the collection entitled, *The History of the Growth of Heaven*. Nonetheless, each of them acquired an inchoate biography and a brief, independent "half-life." This is how I partly described them in those far-off days of the early 1970s: Julio Hernandez "is a jailed Puerto Rican poet, born on the Lower East Side of New York in 1967...Hernandez like Miguel and Julio like my father..."; Peter Boone is "an ex-beatnik who became a sort of mystical fascist in Vietnam or somewhere else. Peter Boone is dead. He was accidentally killed when a bullet struck Garcia Lorca. They were linked by an umbilical cord 30 years long"; Alice Henderson-Codrescu, whose name I borrowed shamelessly from my wife, "is the woman in man...maybe the most unknown woman ever"; and Calvin Boone is "a Dominican monk, kin of Peter." To this day I have no idea if any of them would have survived the climate of our poetry culture. Over the years, I have invented other poets, some of whom lead a modest existence still in literary magazines. None of them, however, are as spectacular or as violently lyrical as my first four.

1. Julio Hernandez

From a Trilogy of Birds

in birds is our stolen being. from summer to summer
they carry on my destruction, more obvious
as i get closer to death.
in the kitchen powerful lights stay on at night
watching the summer passage of birds.
the sea contains
their thick excrement, our longing to fly,
the sea changes color.
weak ships over the water.
i am seasonal.
i offer poisoned lights to passing birds
through the guarded door of the kitchen.
it suddenly opens.
i catch the sea when it is taken away
by disciplined clouds of birds.

A Thing

it's useless to think of myself in medieval terms,
i'm not a saint, i shamelessly enjoy the meat of the prison
when it is well cooked, i'm proud
of my friendship with the librarian
who gets me *the village voice.*
i have a weak memory.
there is only one thing which keeps me
from loving this jail,
that is don quixote
when he comes to my window
and brings me postcards of ugly spanish girls

i'm careful with my dreams of death,
they should not slip into my comrades'
nights,
take the place of their erotic dreams.
—a real jailer is needed for this—
paolo sleeps with his mouth wide open,
mario's left hand hangs from the bed.
i could be free if i let go for a second,
put death in their dreams.
oh dogs of silence,
i need you, señor

The License to Carry a Gun

to andrei codrescu

they will forever refuse you the license to carry a gun
but i am a gun and paolo and john and grazzia
(remember her forked tongue?)
the license to carry a gun is a license to be.
patricius, brutus, don quixote come naked
to my mind vs. target!
they're full of shit by daylight
but when lights go out in these cells
they are my loaded darkness,
my license to carry a gun.

Partiti Sunt Vestimenta Mea
Miserunt Sortem Contra Me ad Incarte
Cla a Filii a Eniol
Liebee Braya Braguesca et Belzebuth★

games of cards are such that they create women
through subtle winds of chance and sweat
on foreheads; chance this time
is given to creation, of a female sort.
oh how their eyes are big, imprisoned players
when from his cards the winner gets a woman,
fucks her, right in front of the others.
she bears no fruit but nothing is wrong,
they think. at dawn
the guards take all the cards away.

★Incantation for luck in cards used by witches of the
14th century.

there is an orange rotting on the table
closer to freedom than i ever was.
i'll throw it away soon, its smell
gives me the same sweet hallucinations
i had when i was holding a gun.
orange of sun, my useless state of mind.

Epitaph (1)

julio hernandez does not lie here,
he lies in your grave

2. Peter Boone

Food

istanbul is a terminal city.
miles away from the stomach of greece.
the goats and the milk
are one sea away.
but my love is integral,
round like an orange on the bed table
of my youth
inches away.
there is something so sexy
about cleaning the filthiest streets in the world.
now holiness at hand
i can proclaim the end of an era,
i can proclaim my fevered body
the king of all beginnings.
soul-dirt falls here
opening a path in the beard of the saint.

Winter in Istanbul

such is the loneliness here.
the birds over some town in new jersey
try to imitate airplanes
and fall dead in the snow.
can't think of anything that bad.
outside the window
a moving theatre.
images of my previous winters.
a play called
freedom.
it isn't death or loneliness.
it's my capacity to wonder
fading in the dawn of the bosphorus
along with my taste for strange politics.
i should invent a woman
to shoot me with her fresh body
of winter.
farewell, black emigrant fantasy,
you who wear sunglasses at night
defending your emigrant body.
our winters meet here.
you make the birds bearable.

Shop

they sell meat flowers in that
crazy shop across the street.
it's a feast called
the menacing babies of future events.
music from somewhere.
there is a meat flower in the piano.
this sale must run intricate ways
like illegal ammunition.
hungry turks.
in their caffeine mystery
the silent secret of...
that one, over there,
one hand on his hip,
the other one deep in his pocket
holding a gun.
the meat flower is now in my words
meaning music

All Wars Are Holy

what happened to me.
it isn't only this war in vietnam.
it's the war of my blood,
the small wars in immaculate labs,
the war of children in the flesh of assaba,
the wars in cosmos over the heads of philosophers.
death, magnetic void of my balance,
beloved one of my sanity,
your silk shoes are soft in the dreams of my brothers.
you finish the milk in the glass
of the rebellious husband
and give sleep to his pain-ridden mate.
don't touch me,
i am your holy mouth

Gist

america is healthy. i am healthy
in the body of christ.
the fall of melted metal builds
my spheric soul.
i go first.
my body's laid flat
on the copper table
and pounded up thin like a sheet
to pick up prophecy.
six holes are drilled in my body.
the marketing of this new instrument
is now in the hands of pan.
i am healthy. i wish
that i had one thousand such instruments.

Note

i dream of a blitz-war of sweating teenagers,
fire-fed by black archbishops
unwinding metallic under jets.
instead, this swamp of slow mysticism,
opening windows without breaking them.
the mind yellow.
the wind of malaria
walks in like the heart of asia.
i'm in the arm of some crazy giant
who sleeps.
lazy women piss in the dust behind hutches.
but it isn't quite that awful.
nothing here is quite that awful.
the bombs
call the time for confession
under the sudden moon

Letter to Ezra Pound

the inferno in a bacteria could be covered up
by a handkerchief. this blue scarf
will do.
yet i can't catch myself
in these trembling planes
seated as I am
on the soft bone of little infernos.
the family is at the root.
(not my family,
  since robert is almost
  ten years old,
  a small communist)
the family.
one, like in my vision of holy wars.
one, like in cunt

Second Letter to Junk Jeannee of NYC

now having seen so many smiles sink
into a perfect pattern of unpaid rent
and recently married meat
i want a sparkle of real-
ity. a box of it
if possible. given to me
through the telephone of your genitals
if the brain doesn't hold.
a painful sign of reality
in the name of my guts, my pretensions,
my previous lives,
in the name of 10th street and 9th street,
in the name of cheap cafeterias
and funny immortality.
istanbul? no.
under so many hats,
under elusive ribbons
the scared shit in the heart
must answer.
the scared shit must pop over and flow free.
i sit near that crack in your head
ready to release another blow

Testing. Testing.

whatever you say, paola francesca di virgine,
leader of mute nuns through the candles of my ideas,
whatever you desire.
see, we could turn the water pipes
into lances shields armors and crosses
and any useless offensive paraphernalia
you prefer.
half of my knighthood offers itself to you
in that sentence.
have some meat from my left arm
and all the fish from this paper bag
and my new refrigerator,
conserver of god
and of milk.
i'll stare at your cross if you say so
till i decompose.
the landlord knocks at the door
and steps on my masked face full of moss
turned blue-eyed to the mad cross
of your impertinence.
well, he says.
there seems to be a question as to your existence.
i am happy to answer that
by punching myself in the mouth.

3. ALICE HENDERSON-CODRESCU

Reverse

a poem for rosa luxemburg who lost it all one summer
but next there it was,
on the other side of a gilded german window.

i, too. born on the other side, alongside
an intricate, painful brain,
in the deep snows of the barbarian kingdom,
a state of permanent sorrow.
the horses unmoved in the warm stables.
beat the ground you were born on,
lash it with your later female skins,
screw your breasts into it,
unveil, unearth.
a country of women.
at some depth we find each other, rosa,
i find your profile obsessing hamburg,
moscow and london.
i'm not nervous any longer,
nerves are short and the longest bone in my body
is black, the longest
year in your memory stops short
of witchcraft.
there is alcohol in your blouse,
revolution is alcohol left over,
the countryside is still fermenting it.
tastes like hell.
rosa luxemburg,
i'm cold and new york is a white city.
the warm glove of your assassin's hand
lies on my table,
dinner for a friend

zzzzzzzzzzz

i want to touch something sensational
like the mind of a shark. the white
electric bulbs of hunger moving
straight to the teeth.
and let there be rain that day over new york.
there is no other way
i can break away from bad news
and cheap merchandise.
(the black woman with a macy's shopping bag
just killed me
from across the street.)
it is comfortable to want
peace from the mind of a shark.

Imported Days

some days, like birthdays, are imported
from france, honolulu and bangkok.
you stretch them out by minutes
and enjoy every piece
while buildings bury themselves in the ground.
you row in and out of a mailman,
a cosmic mailman
from the african or indian market of birthdays.
the sky of this has a hole in the middle,
it pours feasts!
never again beyond into the banal

For Marg
So She Could Fuck Again

i want to clean the lover of the dead warrior
take that strangeness out of her
like a poisonous herb
for my hands to remember.

if you lived through the livers of warriors
kneel near those ladies locked in their hearts,
cut the chain between their knees.
clean prayer, lord of thighs,
make your body go past
the black iron balls of the hero,
past the half-eaten subway in the fork of his memory.
the rats and the rain like an envelope.

i kneel and i clean you,
i put back the flame in your cunt
out of my own.
let's move to the rhythm of my body,
over the lordly gold of the dead in the rain

1st Avenue Basics

if you fight guerrilla warfare in a green skirt
down 1st avenue
leave your breasts at home.
that goes for running guns too.
perfumed high-class mouths blow pearl-handled pistols.
these are the basics of 1st avenue.
the beauty in the hand. basics for a new poetry.
then you warm to your heart
kleenex used by maria dolores.
this helps you erase every trace of your passage.

Reverse

the storm outside
must be the kind you read about in the newspapers,
killer of babies and bums.
the kind of rain that goes on in the subway
when i hold on to the coat of a fat man
whose disastrous life
makes me happy

Dream Dogs

years ago it was easy to dream of wolves
and wake up your lover
to show him the blood on your hip.
the wolves had ties
and followed after every sentence
rather polite.
now there are police dogs
using tear gas and the lover next to you
doesn't wake up.

Debts

the onion tears fall from the eyes of saints.
i have to pay or crack open.
life is salty, this room is hot. how i long
to poke a saint in the nose.
bravado, king of non-existent spain
winds by, his face is young and soon he, too
will be a bunch of tears without a face to punch.
i belong to a more subtle *it*, more nervous,
knowing not how to wait, living in a small room
full of blood and of books.
i pay with colored shells, sharpened at ends,
nothing remains coupled for long.
the tears are spent and our fathers were
11 years old when we got born.
then war came as a proof that neither spain
nor kingdoms do exist.
the tears are sperm. the knife in the purse
is insane.

I Visit Brooklyn with a Queen in Mind

and there, sir, comes a rehearsal of history
when the rings turns purple on the finger of the queen.
she takes off in a halo of pain,
sick like a lemon and stumbling
over the kosher butcher shops of this area.
throughout the earth everywhere
she is accused of witchcraft and death.

her body is well known to many men of her time
and it hangs over them like a seal,
it marks them for delivery.
another seal, smaller, moves inside her seal,
it is secret and hot.
what queer history floods us, sisters.

take matches, for instance, they have been
the closest to your dying flesh
and yet we don't know one another.
the matches light the stove,
the food is quietly cooking.
guard the virginity of brooklyn.
no matter what it holds it is sick.

Poem for Kyra

paradise too is a schizophrenic slum,
a holy octopus with rooms to let
and the four rooms on the left are taken,
it smells as if they are frying angels in there.
in here you smile,
cheat the barefoot goddess at dice,
she doesn't know any better
she's busy unbuttoning your shirt,
feeling your thigh.
you lean on her breasts,
you're maybe ready to die or maybe
it is only dice you're going to play.
for the sheep no danger.
unless you go farther
or take me with you.
then paradise: a thousand strong women
armed with flamethrowers and loaded pussy
storming the streets of the world

4. CALVIN BOONE, OSD

Dear Editors:

The Monk is American, he is wheat treated Bethlehem steel
out of Brother Antoninus' unsaid brotherlies,
all the wasted brotherlies...
He is presently a New Hampshire Monk
of the Dominican Order of Monks,
he is fat. May the blessed Willows pray on his lousy
attempts to the writing of his soul.
Find him care of the Lord's dear
Andrei Codrescu, 3779 25th Street,
San Francisco 94110.
What those numbers mean is no less
than the World,
may Peace answer your knowledge of me,

Calvin Boone
New Hampshire

The History of the Growth of Heaven

As a funny monk one is never sure where
the wind blows the candelabras over the heads
of Fathers at work,
the light of Purgatory.
The funny monks are at the flanks of cheese
and wine, it helps redemption
to savour out the scales of the cell's
square gated window.
I suppose this in a way is a Revolutionary speech,
monks against Fathers or the monk inside Father's
account of the monk.
Good journey then to the illuminati
who set their heavy paws into the highway, drifting
to the wind. Outside,
the fences grow the crazes of a giant ferry

To the Virgin as She Now Stands to the Monk After a Beatles Movie

This is no cell, Holy Woman,
this is a lookout into the shape of that boundless forgery,
into the outline of the Devil's face
when the smog opens up to let us view
the rugged cliffs of his face.
This, of course, is a Monk's crossview
of the book between the legs of naked ladies,
those splinters of you
who go to the movies by themselves
to make love in the dark.
For a flash the singer reaches out on the wire
of your Presence, through the screen,
it hurts to see the waste.
Paralysis of upper vastness, Virgin,
caste out, caste in
of my race.
The terror of your cunt is the beauty of your face.

Faith Relearned

A letter to Father Vietch

Faith is the evidence of things I've wasted,
the evidence of things not seen
maybe the canals of Amsterdam could tell you
where I've been all these years:
partly behind my shoulder blades
scratching the skin's illusion of secret showers,
partly fighting an ancient war,
partly trying to fit a rug on this floor,
Woolworth's, $9.95, no good,
and partly monking in my cell:
the cheese they feed you here muffles your yell,
its holes let in the others',
its holes look out of you:
the things they've seen inside my night
draw blood from the hinges of lovers,
from the owls of Holland at night.
What I see through my cheese holes is
that view the crucifix has
from inside the iron shirt of the Knight
as he bops past crazy windmills

My Next Book

My next book will have a poem for each
Saint dropped by the Church,
33 poems in all,
the longest one for Saint George
who was the longest man in the world when added
to the end of his lance.
I will put a little cross by each poem
meaning "here lies,"
a very deceptive move since no one
will lie in there,
no one, not even the Monk
who will be out thinking of girls
what are poems?

The Sin of Wanting a New Refrigerator

Sin is impervious
to past transmutations
yet this is how it happened:
I desired
the bareness of my cell to open
in the vaster bareness of a new refrigerator,
it,
   the refrigerator,
having come all the way from the First Avenue of my
New York days,
from the fruit stand of the dark
fat merchant.　He opened it up
in another Universe: the milk bottles inside
lit up like Angels. First Avenue
refrigerated. I was a penny short
and I still am.
They tell me here that new refrigerators
are forbidden, oh
that penny had in it a sin
as elemental as the copper
it was made of

More about Poems

I want to write down the life
that could be my life if I insisted
if I pulled up a corner of the cloth to let the lady
with the groceries
have a look at my cock,
flash of storks running errands for God.
I want to perfect a partial view
through a hole in my cloth,
a slanted recording, a window hangup,
not mindful of the undistorted door,
of the remarkable way.
I ought to repair my life with the grease of Poems:
the bourgeois at war with the monk.
Oh, the volume of the devil's lease!

The Indecent Assumptions, the Slaughter Songs

For Ignatio de Loyola

This is vengeance.
Everything that moves is vengeance or else
is a lost face. A lost bet,
a Tibet for the aged, for the slippery
rock foot.
At eighty, the age of youth for most trees,
I will begin the writing of my soul,
of the way it was set in place by a hand more precise
than a lover's.
Oh, inaccurate lovers Oh, washing machines!
The upside down face
of the turn of the century.
The turn of horseshit into bullshit.
Vengeance. Your dish, Ignatio,
seasoned with fried simpletons,
with Knights of the Book.
They thought you will hand it to them.
Oh, God, their Bible, oh, Azvoth, their Kalevala,
Odin, their Mein Kampf,   (Their: Mein)
Oh, Buddha of the Mountain, their little Red Book,
little, no matter how little,
but give it to them.
Maybe my avenging head pulling at the end of the hook
will resume its inventions,
will open up as their Book
of the indecent assumptions,
of the slaughter songs

Gifts of Percussion

For Sister Sue

Wong, goes the bell in the head of the maid:
That fool under my window again!
WONG, goes the fool,
and I know what he means 'cause I was there
when the town fell like a soft cupola over the market place.
Squashed cheese, the sideway face
of the clock screamed.
WONG, just an earthquake!
This brother warns you, Sister Sue,
this earthquake of love will shake you out of your clothes.
WONG, goes the God of your foes!

The Status of the Monk

is not moveable
though your block might be getting worse
and the crickets are moving out. From porch to porch
the twisted ladies have
turned their knitting needles on themselves,
housewife collage.
A people's militia to meet the needs of love.
But I have nothing left to hate,
I remain medieval
no matter what you do to me,
perched on myself like an endless tapestry,
God put his suitcase down to rest on it.
The women try to guess its contents.

About Photography

I hate photographs,
those square paper Judases of the world,
the fakers of love's image of all things.
They show you parents where the frogs of doom
are standing under the heavenly flour,
they picture grassy slopes
where the bugs of accident whirr twisted
in the flaws of the world.
It is weird,
this violence of particulars
against the unity of being

A Programme for the Double Barrel Life When It Hits

Mystically I live on two planes at once
magically I am the two holes of a double barrel gun
threatening to blow me into space.
This is almost true.
The church, the state, the typewriter, the police
are about to kick me out of the world:
the arrogant benevolence of public murder
wiggles loose from lunchcounters,
the devil's toes on the brakes
and my hairy arm.
I would give in
if they left me the whole of my memory,
that dear bone, my flash of life
to uncork at sudden times without warning.
They won't leave me a thing

Attempt to Spell, Incantate and Annoy

May his eyes go on unblinking
and his ears from bells unhurting
may he go the way of wires...
I can't write spells, I'm a monk.
One is constantly expected to write about his environment,
the melting stuff, the mood of his sins,
the geology of the billionth of a second,
I am even supposed to confess my environment
to an asthma struck intermediary of a not-so-instantaneous God,
do you, Holy Ones, suppose
that we are made of thick flesh, rawhide, penicillin,
or is the Confessor really Nylon Man
when he chooses to rip open his ecclesiastic cloth
and go chasing after bank robbers?
I had to put this heresy down on paper
this poem is a heretic environment
how do you confess it?

The First Icon with Gun

Flemish style, late 17th century:
the Virgin holds a gun
not the baby.
Artist, unknown.

Igni Natura Renovatur Integra
(Nature Is Completely Renewed by Fire)

One way to be honest
about the general outlines of the billions
of things that happen to me every second
is to be someone else,
a cowboy, perhaps, just arrived in town,
riding three solid principles bolted to his gun.
It's a damn bore
living in infinity like an ex atom

Junk Mail

Junk mail. A gun for a dollar.
This one-dollar deal has changed the face
of all I thought was mine,
and it still cries from the enormous pain
of being screwed inside my shoes,
made to reside upright,
both eyes directed into the heart of "Daily News"
and snow will be here soon.
The stamp stares me down with "Man on the Moon."
I smell the blades of cold
travelling this side of mail without zip code,
glued to the wide phantoms of cars going out
of style. My snowed in prayers will relieve my heart
of bombs and rifles.
For a while

Stupor at the End of May

What some mistake for me meditating
is a giant stupor with a black hood
sitting cross legged at the end of May, counting
the days till Christmas.
Stupor, flat and simple, the overture
to the large thoughts of the Rectory cow
underfed but happy in her
buzzard shadow

The Hymn of Pan the Flower

The Flower from "to flow," the One who Flows,
Pan the Flow Head, the scented
demiurge who lives inside his pipes, there is
enough room to stretch in if you're his guest
and look at the music wind flowing above your head,
an exact translation
of Capricorn, the stars
of the Goat blowing his pipes' image of you.
There is precision in the process,
there is no boredom

Sarrasin's Wealth Song

boo hoo hoo and boo ha ha
seeing him shit you'd think that he's ready
to enter the heavens holding a cow
by her teats.
this is my cow. and see this, god:
i'm busy; the welfare of chickens,
mushed corn for the rabbits, grease
for the axe and check the balls
of my horses.
i'm a bread maker besides.
so am i. let him go,
he's a busy man.
boo hoo hoo and boo ha ha

Howdy

Before I was a monk I had a cat.
She was darker than Buddha, the great, the elementary.
Actually she was black
and she liked bad wine which she licked
from my glass when I went out
looking for girls.
Her drunk look was of drowned dogs,
of sorrowful junk,
she had seen my brother François
hung from his laces outside his Lady's castle.
From the height of her whiskers it looked like the facts of
        heaven.
Now I'm a monk and Howdy,
'twas her name,
peeps backward into my mouth from a ceiling
of frosted eternity.
The bad wine links us like a birthday feeling

Souls Looking for Bodies

The pregnant women are jealously guarded by their Angels,
perched over them like moist blossoms,
fighting the Souls come to enter.
If the Angel sleeps
the Soul enters.
There is no real choice,
only the sudden loss of vigilance

The Ghouls of Candlemas

stick to the hollies.
Where did you go from Christmas until now?
I went skiing with my slaves on the Virgin Snows
to prepare for love, for the New
World jutting forth from the sinews of New
Hampshire. In the old days
they had Inspectors throwing out the hollies
from Church, for Candlemas.
Now the ghouls are going crazy with the candles
and our auras flicker

(*for Alice*)

The Holy Grail

When they bring in the Dish
the Cup disappears suddenly for many centuries
and before they get to eat
the king sends everyone looking for the Cup
by which time the Dish is gone.
Lately I've been monking at this.
Why does a grown man write poems?
What's an overgrown monk doing away from God
with a typewriter?
Maybe a grown man builds houses.
What does it really matter
what a grown man does
what a grown man is.
This time the Dish is missing.

Symmetry

Sooner or later
everyone finds out who his Murderer is
and most times it lies in bed next to him
holding him by the murder weapon.
For a monk it is harder to guess,
weapon and Murderer belong to another world:
there are no identities to point out
only reflections.
Sometimes a word blows up like a bomb.

San Francisco
1973–1974

On Organization

Has anyone ever earned the respect of sand?
Cement has.
Anything that can be organized can be made
to respect the organizer.
Organization is the process whereby the organizer
eats the organizable.
Anyone with a big stomach can be an organizer.
Only the indigestible is unorganizable.
Therefore make thee as horrible to eat as boiled
spinach!

Love Poem

And while for the sake of sanity
i would eat any vegetable that isn't moldy or rotten
and any animal that hasn't been dead for too long
i would prefer to just eat you, my love,
your many vegetables and juicy animals

Long Door

A very dreamy self
neither old nor young
comes through the door
holding a razor.
The piano next door clatters.
Ether.
Error.
Long door.

Three Types of Loss

1.

The loss of one's temper in a room with absolutely nobody
to catch it
is a loss of time insofar
as time is the only place things
get lost in naturally

losing things constantly implies
a frequency of loss which when measured
is equal to the wavelength one is on in
relation to the things one loses

action that cannot be translated in loss is the only
action
worth remembering

things doomed to loss meet
and get lost together that much faster

all things have in common a tendency to get lost
it is only human affections that
keep them in place

then there is a person called Mr. Loss
who answers house calls the same way
a doctor does—he is supposed
to diagnose the condition of things
on the move and by inevitably confirming
everyone's worst fears he makes
the condition official

the universe gets lost
and then reappears bathed
in a different light

everything has a place to get lost in
and this certainty makes
most things stay put

since one does not lose what one
does not have
most things make themselves necessary

2.

loss of memory after a sleepless night
implies that the things one could have been
dreaming about were the nails that kept
those memories in place

loss of memory at a certain point of heightened interest
in the thing one can't remember
proves the fact that although this is
a universe of nonsimultaneous phenomena
most things would like to be seen in context

memory disregards context
it is an enemy of experience
therefore unreliable and since
basic memory is a condition of survival
i assume that we survive
in spite of experience

when one forgets as a philosophy
each forgotten thing is raised to the status
of a god (i.e. an objective condition)
and makes everyone else remember
things that they haven't experienced

some memories bring with them brand new
experiences different
than the original contexts in which they occurred
and thus set up the conditions
for brand new memories

most things endowed with memory die

prenatal memory is common property
but it is not
objective

words and pictures are the only
things one can forget at leisure
and look up later

3.

what gets lost in translation
reappears in disbelief

translation is the only form of communication
where loss is practiced
as part of the game

literal translations lose music while
poetic translations lose the original

elements which translate themselves
into other elements
do so at the expense of energy

fat translators are common:
they feed on what they cannot translate

the conscious and the unconscious
are languages in a state of translation
and their respective losses
are the gods

translated in english
most things take off their clothes

things lost in translation
band together symbiotically
and haunt the world

war is an aggregate of losses
through translation

the day is a literal translation
the night is a poetic translation

energies translate without apparent loss
but the use of them
makes up by being pure loss

translation and use are in a parenthetical
relationship

fate is the necessity for translation

Secret Training

The busdriver of the Mission bus at 1 A.M. is a statistician of chance, he computes his run of luck by mentally guessing how many people will get on his bus at each stop. Every time he guesses wrong he chalks it up to the ODDS column; when he guesses right he puts it in EVENS. This way he learns the ratio of occurrence of luck in his guesses and cunningly uses his knowledge to win his way through Las Vegas and Monte Carlo to owning a giant fleet of taxicabs in which he introduces a strange sort of meter that charges passengers not according to miles travelled but to random guesses based on the character, wealth and astrological signs of the clientele; these meters are so accurately timed to the owner's ratio of luck that soon he is rich enough to own an airline but this airline is soon outlawed and the owner put in jail because half the planes crash for inexplicable reasons through sudden streaks of disorder in his relations to chance.

Dream (1)

They operated on my brain. First she cut a round slice off the top of my head and put it aside then she extracted a big piece of brain from the front. She put the top back on and notwithstanding my fears of memory loss she told me to come back next day. In the hallway outside I meet their beautiful daughter who is a dancer. Next day I come back to have my brain piece reinserted. I am given a shot and the top of my head is again cut off. Last night's fresh brain looks refrigerated, an old piece of liver. "IS THIS MY BRAIN?" I gasp. "IT WILL FRESHEN UP AGAIN ONCE IT'S BACK INSIDE YOUR HEAD," she says; they put it back inside my head and they sew the top on. Today I am feeling very weird, very fragile like somebody had stuck the arm of a compass into the center of my head and traced a circle just above the eyebrows.

The Urges

When the urge to strip becomes too much i rub against a tree until it passes back into that core of myself where, besides stripping, urges such as bashing someone's head in, lie still waiting for signs to proceed. Every day i look for incidents. My heart is a bomb with a very fine trigger. Sometimes a hair falls on my nipple and BOOM! the desire to strip or kill is loose and, look out, i've got my eye on you. Rubbing against trees is my only defense against myself. I smell like bark and there is a rustle of leaves when i pass.

Dream (2)

    but first
there is this vast dinner composed
of unnamed and unheard of dishes flying from the sea
through the windows, completely prepared.
there is a hair in the soup, there is
human flesh subtly cooked in. i always
make my own music. for this dinner, in honor of love
and in anticipation of sleep, i spread
my instruments before me. the food makes music
in my mouth and my lovers listen.

Power

Power is an inferiority complex wound up like a clock by an inability to relax. At the height of my power I have to be taken to a power source in the woods where I am recharged. This power source is not actually in the woods: it's in my mother. It hums quietly in her heart like an atomic plant and the place to plug in is her eyes.

Silence

The town is never silent. No matter what time it is there is always someone talking. And if no one was talking the wires alone are enough to wake the dead. When the dead wake, forget about silence! All those rattling bones! And even if the people, the wires and the dead were silent, there would still be the indefinite hum of the blood in all the bodies in all the houses. And this is where I come in with my mouth full of silence. I am the size and the shape of an atomizer filled with silence and when I squeeze my inner springs a jet of spray coats everything with the shiny lacquer of silence. In this way I resemble snow but I am more like a self-conscious singer.

On Translation

The Mass creates. The systematic mind or Form misunderstands this creation and makes it Form. Form, in its turn, is sold back to the Mass who misunderstands it and makes it Mass. The misunderstanding of Mass to Form creates the two-party system and the misunderstanding of Form by Mass creates the middle class. These two varieties of Misunderstanding describe, at any given moment, the exact state of the culture. The exact state of the culture is what we call *the worst*. *The best,* on the other hand, has no relationship to the actual state of the culture because it is involved solely with the future. The translator then has two choices. He can translate the best in which case he will have no fun because the future is uncertain therefore serious. One can only laugh at what's solidly here. And he can translate the worst, which is what I do, and be forever amused.

Biographical Notes

my biography
in the absence of facts,
rests on shaky ground

every day
i add thousands of new entries
to my biography

without me
my biography
is *your* story

when made into a play
my biography
speaks with an accent

when alone
with my biography
i give up life

you
are
in my biography

the pictures that go with my biography
haven't yet been taken

De Natura Rerum

I sell myths not poems. With each poem goes a little myth. This myth is not in the poem. It's in my mind. And when the editors of magazines ask me for poems I make them pay for my work by passing along these little myths which I make up. These myths appear at the end of the magazine under the heading ABOUT CONTRIBUTORS or above my poems in italics. Very soon there are as many myths as there are poems and ultimately this is good because each poem does, this way, bring another poet into the world. With this secret method of defying birth controls I populate the world with poets.

Grammar

by mistake, one day, i unplugged grammar, the refrigerator of language, and all the meats of prejudice began to rot

grammar is plugged into the wall of our minds and if i concentrate long enough i can still feel my mother's deft fingers inserting the prongs

i can, for that matter, also remember trying to put my cock through a noun and ending up fucked by a mysterious "it"

there was a man who spoke in complete sentences and one day he was run over by a train

translation can make what comes "after" come "before" and thanks to this i am capable of filling in endless forms with a smile

i have a dim view of commas when i walk

the cannibal group i belong to is presently engaged in wiping its many mouths of dripping pieces of syntax with the long towel of my mother's skirt

&

i hate
everything that moves faster than my body because
everything that moves faster than my body
does so by a cheap trick

Here

The Earthfault we stand on is nobody's fault
just as the spine dividing me right now
divides no one else.
On second thought we are standing on the wife
of a famous earthquake,
a dame known as Joan,
daughter of a mad church builder,
thief of silver watches
and inventor of some musical terms.
Lying down with the wife of an earthquake.
A red haired ball of flame.
Oh I love you more than you could know

5 Ways of Saying the Same Thing

the carbon of everything that ever went on meets the manuscript
of the future; they shake hands in passing and throw the body
(me) down the well

two total strangers meet inside me, fuck, and then i am born

two lips, peaceful and at ease with each other, belonging to the
same person, meet two other lips just as peaceful and an ambiva-
lent violence develops, out of which comes blood and, some-
times, a whole war of bodies

the straws in a squashed straw hat preserve the footprint faithfully
long after the squasher has vanished until the straw rots and it is in
this same way that i am holding on to my childhood

dessert as a reward or carrot dangled from a stick at the end of a
horrible dinner shines like god through my life—but i like dinner
better—i hate dessert

we drown in you, california fog, like two lips in the foam of a
chocolate soda!

Designs

the zodiac towel wipes the hands
of the zodiac killer
and burns up. the zodiac towel
was designed by peter max. the
zodiac killer was designed by god.
both of them, god
and max, are prefigured
in the zodiac
as very great designers

Dollar Air

I have a bag with a silver dollar in it.
If you take away the dollar
a field of anger remains
steaming your eyeglasses.
This kind of violence which accompanies dollars
everywhere, even to the movies,
grows roots when left alone and then
becomes a tree for suicides

& Power

Power, this
coil thumping around,
obeys me like a stove.
I dig your half drawn claws at the shutters
of my daily emergence.
And your eyes on the roof
of my mouth counting the chipped
constellations.
And your finger on my back tracing
an old woman picking long rags
from the garbage cans
swaying in the wind.

And in her memory God knows
what awesome riches
I possess.
Kneeling with you
is being
everywhere

A Game

those random sparks from telegraph poles, horse
shoes on pavements, beards
on fire
put me to sleep.
i've been counting the sparks in my blood.
two sparks for "peasant"
nine sparks for "aristocrat"
many sparks for "dopefiend."
from sparkling graves the noble heads are popping out.
behind this botany of skinny sparks i see fat flames
cooking potatoes on the hothouse roof

Dollar Dance

the poor loves his music
at the expense of god whose music
i also love

exotic fish in the frying pan
weird women on the black satin sheets
a bum at the window
                                    me

imitating
the simple mute joy of a dead dollar bill
for the visiting grocery list

Rain

Dreaming I am in Egypt trying to convince
the cells in my brain that they are birds
and they will leave me some day
to find mates! The bird flocks
of my life leave my cigarette and write
big S's on the ceiling. Oh perched madonna
over the cold beef, forgive me the plotting
of this place. The instructions are
go drown yourself!

Why Paint?

the wrathful mastodon is tearing
up the dictionary while we are having
dinner in the next room with unknown
animals sitting both across
from us and in the plates. why should
anyone bother with a portrait?
if you are painting us, forget it!

The Worst Poems Make the Best "Poems"

If my manner of song disturbs the dead the living
and the near dead it is because
near the dead end you can't dance.
I dance to the noise of market places and to the jingle
of coins in the pocket of a subway cop
I dance with the quiver of tomatoes
slipping into paper bags
and I dance to the tune of a day when I will be dead
and the farts of a cow near my tomb
will drive me bots

Music

in music we are sick lovers
whipping ourselves like bums whipping
the windows of the liquor store
like junkies whipping their arms to make
the veins rise. not all music
is like that. only the music
i live with.

War & Peace

your nipples go to war
in strange apartments. later
we share the loot. rich corpses exit
tongue first from the well of your face.
we strip them down to tiny red
atomic pills. their gold teeth
give us hope.
on the mined fields of your skin
men blow up like frogs with straw
up their asses. someone
is parachuting from the sky
with our clothes.

Junk Dawn, NYC

greeks mounted on needle points
drop through asia minor
into our veins via new york
and the room fills with the pure
products of my imagination like a rag
with gasoline. for no particular
reason the floor is sooty and the small
buddhas crouching in the corners
are sick with a fragrance
of hair. there is nowhere to go
save inside yourself: there everything
is slightly demented and free

Some Days

some days instead of breakfast
i have visions. i see myself trapped
behind a heart without windows. i cry
for eggs until i'm knocked against The Egg

Politics

you are in a barbed land and you are NOT dying.
the claws of the grass are bent
inwards. likewise the trees are tearing nothing
but their own hearts. everything holds in
the bleeding meat of self-injury.
surrounded by protection from each other
we have left the inside
vulnerable.
it is the walls i hate with all my heart
and those who, dead inside,
have built them from their own disfigured corpses

Hop Scotch

i never understood hop scotch. all the
squares between the Mighty and his legless
servants have always
seemed filled. but not always
by the best. corporate crocodiles
wiggled on the wet tiles. whenever
i lifted my leg i felt an unimpeachable
desire for chocolate. i had
as a child been hampered by a burglar
alarm between my legs. this
has not changed. i am still alarmed
at the state of the world.
the squares look the same.

Saturnian Dilemma

i am a vision looking for a way out of
my head. i have a head in every window
of an endless row of houses. i have a hand
in every refrigerator. moonlit
french fries drive me to frenzy. i have
envisioned telling the truth which is what
my body consists of. every time
i have been stopped
by my appetite

Your Country

in the country of eight hundred different kinds
of flying machines
i put on my blue gloves.
in other countries i have
put on my red shoes.
it is only in your country
i take off everything.
it is only in your country
i empty my pockets.

Looks from Money

ah, money, you colorless flat shit growing
from the uniqueness of this day like a grandmother
out of the pear tree,
what kind of dreadful holes are you boring
in the small of my back

money touched by gary cooper and by adolf hitler
oh money in balloons
take your hair out of my life broth
out with your guts and be gone

there is a train filled with blind birds
going broke

breasts fall from broken piggybanks
contracts are drawn in the park and photography
lays waste my mind

my bruised neck
in a thousand billfolds

"The Woods" at Midnight

i see a man with a whistle between his lips
perpetually calling the police. i see
myself laughing so hard the windows
shake and the stuffed birds fall
from the mantel to become fruit
in "the woods"
at midnight. i see also a vast
bowl filled with hot water out of which
fingers emerge clutching
at my throat. "the chalice
is full with the pregnant host"
no doubt but i'm lost

A Serious Morning

being serious is a
perversion of natural form
an extension of a bruised baby hand
behind which towers the tilted needle
of a dim father's body.
and the bees of his eyes dying with contempt.
i'm awash with the serious tools
of a mysterious trade.
the hushed windows of my receding house.
the power lines humming death wishes.
the dry wines in the palm of the hand.
if i were to laugh my ass off at all this
i would take up
a form of politics that ends
with a cheerleader licking the wounds
of my machine gunned body

Telegram

dear wolfgang:
the asshole of the devil
smells like fried chicken

Old Photo

these men, the last workers on the world's
crookedest railway, stand up like columns
under the genius of a red star.
there is something pitted against and pushing
their stucco houses out of the temporary landscape,
something pitted against their daughters'
black hair, an opening up
of the terrors in the spare junipers
of mount tam.
hard oak canes are laid across the tracks.

The Police

they are stripping the fur of the police
with these two eyes of mine.
a handful of witnesses bathe in wine
and the nymphlings shriek.
this is a scene from "history"
where it often happens that inside one's genes
is lodged a horror of police
like a horror of cats.
on which side of my emerging beard
should i start to stir?
oh right here. here is a place of
fur flakes, soft like your ass.
is this cavemoist making new bones?
until resurrection no one knows.
i like it that way.

The Imagination of Necessity

there comes a time when everything is laced
the water you drink   the words you speak
your manner of turning   of being
& the substance
is undefinable   coloratura of a
scale moving backwards into embryo tonality
which is not so bad when you possess a technique
of encounter or a professional philosophy
when you are a baker or an expert
lover   which is terrible when you live
with a rope around your neck a flower in your cock
a windlike disability   a flight pattern
drawn in the wrong sky in the wrong season
ducks sucked out of migration into disarray
oh concentrate then!   if you can
on the mystery ingredient   imagine your body
a spoon stirring the sugar at the bottom of a vast
cup of tea & the melting strings of sugar
on which the angels of hot water
climb with ferocious aptitude   what this imagining
gives   besides a headache   is an ease
of penetration a fluidity in entering strange
houses   a lack of weight in taking what's not yours
but fits you   & good luck

The Origin of Electricity

What I look at amazes me. What I love scares me. Sometimes I'm a nun being whipped in public view. Sometimes I whip myself privately in a little cell set up for the purpose. Sometimes Communism seems to be on the march sometimes I am marching all alone through the quicksands. The complexity of my situation is further enhanced by a little black screen on which the intimacies of the great are shown in exasperating detail. Now if I could live in a state of perpetual coma I could blame my imagination. But I am a perfect absorber of detail. The shine on someone's shoes, if properly framed, can repeat itself ten thousand times unhindered in the recesses of my brain. My capacity for moving by echo-location is notorious but only if the object emitting the sound is the only object within a ten-mile perimeter. For that which I am there is no name but for that which I helped create the name is Electricity.

Us

Oh I believe that all of us real poets string pickers
all of you great geniuses of my changing crystals
all of you and all beasts
have been growing hungry from a fast in us.
Now now here is the presence of mind
needed to stand up in the refrigerator and turn on the light
spouting from the butter, eerie eggs
of mind presence snowing near the gardens.
Dear God, Cauliflower & Broccoli are so Beautiful Together!
And the frozen ducks in the cracked cellophane pushing
a slice of pizza into the side of a clam can!
And the cheese singing!
Oh I believe that all of us
are ready!

Face Portrait

I am a man of face like another is "a man
of position" or "a man of hair." I take
things at their face value and the weight
of this world slides off
my face like a skier over snow. I live
through my face like others "get through
the day." It is not a particularly handsome
face, rather a gross sensual
barrage meant to take the breath out of you.
I imagine death as an epiphany of my face
in which a glow of dying roses clutched
in a diffusion of angles by discarnate hands
descends upon my eyes
and breaks them loose.
While the garters of divine ladies
snap and escape with my ears.
Still, I am alive and in this season of my face
there is the joy of sinning without surgery!

Work

at night the day is constantly woken up
by exploding dream objects
until all our days are tired
and collapse on our hearts like loud
zippers breaking in the middle.
i sleep in the daytime with my head on the piano.
i sleep at night too standing on the roof.
i sleep all the sleep that is given me plus
the sleep of those who can't sleep and the sleep
of great animals who lie wounded
and unable to sleep.
i'm dead tired from the work everyone does
ceaselessly around me, from the work the morning
crowds are going to do after they are thrown up
by the thousand mouths of toast and cologne
into the buses and subways,
from the work the plants do to get water
from the labors of beasts looking for meat
from the labors of speaking replying writing
from the work going on inside me with a million
greedy cells beating the shit out of each other
from the work of the sun turning around
and the earth turning around it.
i'm tired in general and sleepy in particular.
i have a great desire to move elsewhere.

New York

The street of this strange metropolis...
Frozen spaghetti, fear of ghosts...
The scarred pavements
have a very eloquent texture
of bums woven with empty bottles and soot,
an ancient tapestry.
On this curious mattress one bounces looking for sex.
Layers and layers of sex
for each layer of you... Tongue overlaps
with ten thousand other tongues,
genitals are enmeshed in so many other genitals
that a ball of flame floats permanently around the city.
If you think this is rough
you don't know the heart of it because it's
silky and funny and feels
like the breeze of hereafter

Tête-à-Tête

my body, spill-proof but not quite,
is full of grinning groceries. my liver
dreams of paté. my heart
makes the soup red. my head
stuffs itself with birds. even
my fingernails look good in jello.
the trick is to bring in each
dish at the right time in the dim
candlelight. the trick
is to surprise your guest with the ease
with which you delve into
yourself

Trains

trains run on emotion not
good advice. the southern pacific
runs on a wet appetite. the trans-
siberian is loaded with boxes filled
with the tears of russians
going to hell. romanian rail-
roads run only in the rain and not
every time. on french
trains women give birth. and the rails
themselves are licked shiny every-
day by the tongues of museum
curators

A Grammar

i was dead and i wanted peace
then i was peaceful and not quite dead yet
then i was in my clothes
and i took them off and then
there was too much light
and night fell
then i wanted to talk to somebody
and i spoke ecstatically
and i was answered on time in every language
in a beautiful way
but i felt unloved and everyone
came to love me

still there is something running
and i can't catch it
i am always behind

The Best Side of Me

tomatoes squashes and cauliflowers intrigue me immensely
with their lewd proposals
and their making the stability of my appetite burst
with the lust of their red yellow and white chewiness
you're chewy, i'm looney.
i dream of soft furry things with inward claws
lodged in my brain
which open when it rains.
then whole cities built around a globe of waving squash.
we float backwards into early tickles of consciousness.
faces pull through complicated threads of greasy smiles.
my friend peter chewing on his model airplane.
the stretched frown of my tomato nanny.
if i ever walk out of this dream
my work is all over. my body releases
the captives from ten thousand labors.

Poetry Paper

the great poets are not in the language but in business because what poet can make cut production costs equal infinite compassion, offhand, in a matter of fact way and in a tone that excludes misunderstanding? not only do the great poets now sit outside language manipulating the heart but also the great readers of poetry who, stunned in the past by the printed page, are now free to have dinner and board a bus in the company of sheer poetry with not a thought for their own failings which, quite apart from their bodies, they now take to the doctors to get fixed? in our time, we elevate details to the power of numbers, to the place where concrete representation has flown the coop, and one day we will see ourselves translated in machinery and this, thank god, will be the day when i will unscrew my head with the silence of my surroundings and go to sleep forever.

Sea Sickness

dancers strapped to canoes is
what the morning brings. they are tied
to a perpetual dance.
hooded folks in lighthouses
count on their fingers as the day
gets brighter. everywhere
dancing is either law
or crime. i have no particular
taste for this world. i am looking
for an utterly still completely
dead hotel.

Early Fix

It's been like this every morning:
a clock and the pattern
is irretrievably set
by an authoritarian hand pressed
palm down on your forehead.
All day you walk with the map
of someone's life shining from under
the roots of your hair.
Since everyone (as if you cared)
assumes now that your head
is a hand
you go on pouring coffee through the lights
of your brain.
Every thought is a missing ship.
The little babies in the pictures turn
into voracious gypsies
reading your script

Opium for Britt Wilkie

The beautiful swimmer the extremely shy
opium eater touches his hat
in homage to the great pool lying
still at the feet of the crow. The
snow on his hat says
something to me but I am a weapon
with a small vocabulary
hanging from a deerhorn rack. And
then he plunges into the blue water into
our afternoon. Oh hello there. We are
squeezing a string of smoke to cause our melo-
dramatic hearts to ripple up and down
the spine of the world. But he just
swims on sending a slight metallic shock
through us. OK. When we will meet
again he will be swimming back having
brought a big wet clock with him from the other
side of this home

Manifesto

It's opium we need not truth.
Unless we are and we are morally pinned to the wall
with a gold stake. I am
pinned to your forehead, Karl Marx, like a
butterfly to a skirt.
The one way out is through blood, your
blood. Here, surrounded by the serenity
and transparence of opium
we sail toward the island of your blood.
When we stop we experience night.
As we go on the light of day bathes us.

Alberta

When Alberta swims the whole night in the creek behind the house where I sit counting the rooms, I want to send owls in the branches above her with the results of my count. 13 rooms, Alberta, 13 rooms! Or maybe a thousand! But what owls, indeed what beasts, can last the impact of her smooth, wet body leaving a trail of warm dark men in the phosphorescent water...Two fishes mate in the depression between her breasts! Waiting their turn, all the other creatures in the creek are emitting a light that messes up my count. How many rooms did I say? Then she speaks from my faucet when I drink and the glass of water in my hand shimmers with an invisible lust. At the end of all these rooms, at the end, indeed, of all rooms, there is Alberta swimming on and her strokes inside my bloodcells culminate in light, in small blue explosions.

Good Morning

sometimes when they shut off the faucets
i think of chinese mailmen
how they must feel holding
birds full of letters.
i would like to walk with them
into the small
circumcisions at the top of houses
through which hands protrude waiting
for telegrams.
because this is a country of telegrams
we emerge from holding shocked doorknobs
between our knees

Opium for Archie Anderson

I am home eating a heart A very slow
heart! A languishing pregnancy
pushes its lazy baby through the tenth
year! We hear the news under-
water Morsel after morsel
of hysteria. Look I am home with the
bride She is lying
on a bed of artichokes with her heart hovering
over her overripe belly And
she hasn't been speaking for years except
to me! And
I lie! I lie a lot! I will
eat this heart I will go out and tell Look
I ate a heart I will
do it again! I will
eat your heart if only you could
be seized with such miracles! If only
you could rot so graciously on a bed
of artichokes If only you could
drive me south! Drive me deaf! If
you could bubble like mineral waters! If you
could walk up my ladders! Human
ladders!

Crossed Hands

One day our noses will be in heaven
while our arms will roast in hell, the body
is a watch composed of moralities with different
places of encampment. Take then
this body home with you and love it in general
like you love your grandmother.
She has long since been entered in a log
of lovestains on a sheet of dark
and with her image we will knot
frantic new bones.
All resurrection must begin right away.

Architecture

"Why not call it Egypt?" (Dick Gallup)

Your pubic hair is the apex of a lovely
triangle rising through each day of my life
to complete a pyramid being secretly built
in my blood.
The mythical import of this construct
is then placed in the perspective of what the dead
are building under the streams, in what
imitations of us are being plotted by governments
in the cheaper materials, in rawhide
and in silver telephones

October 17

visitación! visitación!
i had both my hands on the red telephone!
maría! maría! mother of god!
the cracks in the ceiling are lines in the palm!
my fingers are sweating with blessings!
the honey of the apocalypse is upon your soft body!
maría of the motelroom ceiling!
stars of the red telephone!

October 19

rain blows my eyelashes upwards toward
the spot of light which is my face
which is being circled by a dove.
i am lying under a piano
and your beautiful white feet are on my naked belly.
the rain of the Lord is in my heart.

The History of the Growth of Heaven

"*tout ce qui existe est situé*" said max jacob and one day my situation was such that only a detached, religious and ecstatic perspective could bring home all that i was. since i was nothing in particular at that time i became a monk because it seemed to me that monks had no ego, only visions and a sense of humor. i am still a monk to the extent that this is true. my professional services when i am in robes consist of techniques for sabotaging history with the aid of god. so to speak.

The Good Spirit

the spirit of this room is dead. it was a very good spirit.
it kept the tea warm and it put me to sleep
it fastened our love and it took good care of the heart.
it shone over the lower east side.
1 A.M.: things are unveiled, we are unprotected at night
and i want to plant an insane bomb in my own liver.
so i will never meet my edges again.
if only this disgust would leave me alone.

History

in 1946 there was my mother inside whom
i was still hiding.
in 1953 i was small enough to curl behind a tire
while the man with the knife passed.
in 1953 also i felt comfortable under the table
while everyone cried because stalin was dead.
in 1965 i hid inside my head
and the colors were formidable.
and just now at the end of 1971
i could have hidden inside a comfy hollow in the phone
but i couldn't find the entrance

Breakfast Elegy

ever since the abandonment of courtship
i haven't had a good time in the world   a city
is a bomb in your liver which lets *you*
set the timer   when the sun is out
you don't want to blow up   love love
i am responsible for the welfare of the idiot masses
i carry the darkness of ages on my back
i carry a knife in my boot   a purple water issues
from our genetic taps   what can i say
that does not instantly jell as the sugar in birds
crystallizes in flight

Why Write

i've always looked for joy as a pretext to write
but could not or would not
fall face down upon that knot of pain which seems
to make even the simplest things
a complete and frightening mystery.
this way i have avoided being torn
by the terrific closeness with that heart-shaped weapon
which makes us die. i have left out
important fragments of my life. i've taken only
the juice out of the squalor. i have avoided
loving more than i *could* love.

Eugenio Montale in California

and here where a new life
sprouts into a mild
anxiety from the orient
your words, like the scales on a dying fish,
flash into sunset

Fear

fear is my way
of not being here although
i am afraid of falling asleep for fear
of a frightening thing taking place in my absence.
i am also
afraid of the axe i keep behind the bed hoping
that no one will come in or rather
that someone will
and there will be blood.
sitting there in the dark seeing myself kill
over and over
is not fear,
it is pleasure
though when the awareness of pleasure floats up
and i learn that it is pleasure
i become very afraid.
this new house is fear
of the unknown neighbors stretching for miles
in each direction with only
space for houses with no one in them
space for dark windows over basements filled with fear.
the long stone walk from the door
to the top of the stairs
has three major checkpoints of fear:
the cottage on the right where the spooks sit
on the bicycle chains,
the old jew's apartment with the curtains drawn
over the candle light
and finally the stairs themselves going up
through minor and major stations of fear
which at the age of six are like the days themselves,
long, inexorable.
and now the fear of even writing about fear
the fear of awareness

A Point

This then is the point of my life
(a point not in me or in the middle)
where a light flashes down from the mountain
with a chinese determination
to have my body yield a series
of moral statements.
To say what it feels like to lie.
Or to judge the import of a slashed throat
under the dirty shirt collar.
Or to determine how agreeable the death
of one's mother is
in the dimming business hours.
Later this point becomes me as I
reappear in town peddling a substance
taken from the bodies of flagellant monks

Books

death covers me with fine dust.
i love used fat books. they are
like used fat bodies coming out of sleep
covered with fingerprints and shiny
snail trails.
i wish to read the way i love:
jumping from mirror to mirror like a drop of oil
farther and farther from my death.
but god gives us fat books and fat bodies
to use for different reasons
and less a metaphor i cannot say
what haunts me

Star Book

there are many books about the zodiac
that mirror us. from each
page shines the lion of a yet
unlived day. the best
book is the stars themselves right
before dawn when the chill of your mind
sucks itself home. the summer
of california is the best
binding!

Poem

the supreme test of one's poem
is in the bathtub standing up naked hands
above the head like a gothic christ
and if the picture in the mirror is of a fat
belly swaying between the forks of a black grin
it's still OK! but no poem

Alice's Brilliance

Her brilliance consists in colors. She can sink her teeth
into a nuance from one thousand steps like the Lone Ranger.
She sees rainbows, desert sunsets and Dutch Boy factories
in every drop of water and in this tablecloth. There is
nothing doesn't come to her for therapy because she can,
you see, cure grey desperate people by yanking the veil
from their eyes and revealing the brilliant dazzle even
in the patches of their pants. Everyone is richer for her
presence. Since she came to town we move more graciously,
there is coquetry in the air, the trees bow gallantly. I
don't want to upset my colors over you, buster, says the
traffic cop handing out a rolled papyrus with a ticket
written on it in gold ink and gothic characters. His
pearl-handled revolver sways gently on his curved hip.
The old truckdrivers even exude an air of civilization,
a thin blanket of pink. All the rougher colors gather
by the river and tell violet stories shifting their eyes
like needles in the ochre light. At times her brilliance
attains peaks of perfection and we feel pierced by un-
known and unnamed colors that then stay perched like
vultures on our hearts and defend us against death.

Talismanic Ceremony for Lucian,
March 9, 1971, Intersection Church, San Francisco

since he's not jewish
and he won't get circumcized
or bar mitzvahed

since he's not christian
and he won't get christened
or given first communion

since he's not a baby anymore
and too big to wear
pink and blue pajamas

i now pronounce him a kid

this is a solemn ceremony
in which
his mommy
is giving him back
his umbilical cord

to protect him from this world
with a talisman
from another

this is then a solemn ceremony
in which
his father
is giving him a new name

LUCIAN CODRESCU

to make him the first

Dictated by Alice Codrescu

San Francisco for Whomever

"Whomever," this is for you!
The streets of this beautiful town
bend minds all day long.
They bend them up the hills and then they blow them
down the sparrow sights.
When you open your eyes something else
opens hers.
Cubic miles of raw cotton in pink laundry bags to
swim into.
At the end of a tickle of blue you loaf away.
Your hips pass you by
oh pictures of my life in every window
with faces of new girlfriends
in blue sails flying the turtles
from these red eggs.
There is a storm in your walking motors
and there is the beginning of the world lying ahead

Late Night, San Francisco

so few things to write about
when there is a sky full of the electrical lights of san francisco

stilling the lights in your head from the left
and the sea some two feet away filling the other ear
with the sounds of all the things you ever wanted to say.
the wind the horse thief takes whatever is left over
from that music i cherish inside winelike in the airtight heart.

there is nothing here now.
the whining after the unplugging of the world.

Thieves, Seasons

At the end of summer they burn the house we live in.
See the hooks of a change
bigger than words
clawing at the shut veins in the leaves.
When the thieves come to scavenge
I put your hand over my mouth
not really a mouth.
Only a bowl of fermenting yucca
in the half coconut shell.
Dear Mom,
they've stolen my mouth from under her hand.
Now they can burn
everything. The winter seagulls are already
at the guts of alien carrion. I don't
recognize a thing.
Supreme thieves are in the order of greater events:
they leave a mythical confusion on which we build
our next lives

Bi-lingual

I speak two languages. I've learnt one of them in a trance, for no reason at all, in a very short time, on horseback, in glimpses, between silent revolts. One is the language of my birth, a speech which, more or less, contains my rational mind because it is in this tongue that I find myself counting change in the supermarket and filing away my published poems. In a sense, these two languages are my private day and night because what one knows without having learned is the day, full of light and indelicate assumptions. The language of the night is fragile, it depends for most part on memory and memory is a vast white sheet on which the most preposterous things are written. The acquired language is permanently under the watch of my native tongue like a prisoner in a cage. Lately, this new language has planned an escape to which I fully subscribe. It plans to get away in the middle of the night with most of my mind and never return. This piece of writing in the acquired language is part of the plan: while the native tongue is (right now!) beginning to translate it, a big chunk of my mind has already detached itself and is floating in space entirely free...

Les Fleurs du Cinéma

i would like to throw a net over these moments when i find myself in the position of an accountant, a clerk of the world, in order to capture them for a future window display of objectivity, a box of signatures from a perfectly harmonious space. these moments like certain flowers bloom so rarely that the entire being of the world participates in their detection. cinema is the great fertilizer. often i find myself in a perfectly dark movie theatre being swiftly seized by an involvement with objective substance until the chair under me melts and there, on the vast cinemascope screen, i hear myself breathing a variety of numbers, all perfect, all accurate, all full of the sweetness of the absolute. this casket of numbers inside which my clear body will never decay is then taken out through a hole in eastman kodak into the mind of god whose fodder these bodies are. and that's that.

Evening Particulier

What did you eat? Who did you call? Oh, exquisite asparagus, I lift these tatters of myself to the sorrows of the alphabet and despair of ever being as splendid as you! Neither will I ever be like a piano! Or like an onion! Imagination is my only grace and I am tired of her constant presence!

Port of Call

did you ever have a grey knot topped symbolically with lightning bolts and mounted in the middle of yourself like a pagoda? of course not. but i have. i have the only one in the world or rather i had because i've traded it in for a scarf. this scarf, see, is from god. you can see smears of cheese on it. cheese? yes, god's feet are made of cheese. wherever he walks he leaves smears. that's how he walked upon the waters ... the water went into the holes in the cheese and the whole thing swole up ... like floaters ... rubber balloons. except that they were cheese shoes. the cheese shoes of jesus. well, anyway, that's how i got the scarf but i will trade it to you for a paddle board. do you need a paddle board? no, but i know someone who does ... he'll trade his gum wrappers for the paddle board. do you need gum wrappers? no, i will give the gum wrappers to a tall man ... he knows me. he wants the wrappers because he needs to wrap himself. do you need anything? yes. i need a port of call.

Mail

Envelopes arrive from everywhere and they are filled with earth. In the beginning I suspected that this was a holy sort of ground which, when possessed in large quantity, would allow me to kneel on it and plant a few vegetables. It is nothing but sand. It has the appearance of fertile earth but after a few days it turns to sand. All the drawers and the closets are filled with sand. What disconcerts me is the night which brings with it the sound of the sea as if the great waters were looking for a lost beach. I sleep in my clothes.

Monte Rio

1974 – 1978

Poetry

Poetry is a discourse.
And we, its discouragees.
If it's a world wide depression,
everybody is depressed.
Ah, but try to run a Gipsy
through the ruins of time.
My publisher says:
at some people's readings, the crowd
goes out and buys their books.
At yours, they run out and steal them.
Why would they want to steal
the blackness of my dog, the mouth
of my tomb?
His body, full of morphine, expires
on the cold cement floor of the jail,
his cells are migrating.
Adieu, dumb dog!
Adieu, obnoxious individuality!

January 3, 1976

The Travels of a Vigilante

Here it is: a thousand miles.
Here is the paint, here is the sharp pain.
All this is plain.
Unwrapping red mummies, licking statuary,
breaking glass, kicking their balls...
This was the refrain.
The chorus was armed and the string section
made neat little loops
for their own heads and finished their sections
with suicide.
It was music, it was glorious.
Anarchy wallows in gauze and this was not
anarchy; the world had a floor.
There were no reasons. Only trains.
Trains going back and trains arriving.
It was a time to roll in wet foliage and sever
the persistent past.
We ate up their supply.
We bent their shovels and cut up their cocks.
The holiday was over.
Well, time for more of the same.

Body Blues

What do you body want? Food? Food?
Here, body, have some food. What does
the body want? Coffee? Coffee? Here here
body have some coffee! Outside? Outside?
Let's go! Inside? Pussy? Pussy?
Here body have some pussy! Movies? Movies?
Here here body there there. Didn't you
get enough tit? Why didn't you? What was
the matter with her? Pushups?
Pushups? I'm pushing you up and down
body, what do you want now?
Speak, goddammit!

Casting

My clothes grow dull in the closet.
The men in them grow restless like the sea.
The man in the blue suit is hungry. He walks across
the menu like a lion, hitting his gabardine reflection
in the window, on the neck with a blue glove.
An intelligent romantic fills in my chinese kimono.
His violence, curled like a mandrake at the bottom of a tea cup,
is poised to strike a flying spirochete: an angel.
In my shoes stands the crowd, fresh back from war,
striking for softer roads.
On them falls the shadow of my trousers like a sword
as the silk fold of the night milks itself in a new way.
But I am standing naked, on a rock face, in the moon.
This is my perfect balcony and with the loaf
of French bread in my hand I am now pointing
at the chasm below, where a vast and hideous
animal is hiding: Eat! You mutha! I flex a rubber arm.
This animal, a rich relation, incurring both hope and horror,
swims up: it is the Hat.
Yes, consider simply the business of buying a hat
if you think words get born in a fog:
between the man who buys a hat and the man
who is afraid of his hair
a chasm opens filled with the bodies of a thousand
awkward thinkers, bad athletes, men not ready.
You may look wistfully toward the other side
watching with ill-concealed envy the tall door
closing behind the stark gentleman.
Maybe, one day, you tell your head.
Maybe one day when the lumps in you and the lack
of hair will make the leap inevitable,
maybe then I too will stand under the yellow lamplight
on the rain-wet sidewalk to tell a lonely
war veteran hurrying in his wheelchair toward god knows
what awful supper in the deserted city:
I have joined the bourgeoisie! I can go home now!
which will or will not be sufficient.
You tell your head all these things: the Hat
glows in the window of the chasm below. It has no feelings
so you walk endlessly around its rim.

Without the hat
they will never shoot you for the boredom you bear in your heart!
With the hat, the man in the blue suit will get to eat.
With it, the intelligent romantic will find the mirror
on which he'll squash his angel flat.
With it, the crowd will get to grow fat.
Without it, they will make guerrilla war.
Well, hat or no hat?
So I am naked on a jutting rock.
It would help if I remembered who wore it and when:
then my head will shake my hand and together
we will begin walking up the broken mosaic
of the overgrown path toward the music
where we will be greeted—by the bandstand—with the news
that night has closed up the armories
and we are out of weapons.

To my Heart

I am a cross and the idea
Is to burn twice at the four tips.

All night I work the hoses putting
Out fires in between.

The fires I understand are vices and
The idea comes from my heart

Threatening to stop.
It beats six times and then it leaps

Upward into nothingness. It feels
Like a rehearsal.

I better stop smoking, drinking and rocking
Little dogs on my lap.

I see somebody bigger than the moon
Delve into my affairs.

Somebody's making a mistake.
I may be talking fast but I am only

28 years of age.
Some day I will be all the rage.

Russia or The Weakness of Photography

Over the landscape walk the mailboxes disguised as whores.
We drunks walk into them and maim our pricks.
The snows threaten the idiots with a vast maze.
They will be seeking lifetimes for their hammers.
They will waste their strength pulling sickles out of the necks
of patient Ukrainian peasants, photographed by God.
As the idiots struggle, I will close shop, bid adieu to the super-
market where I stood for the language, I will
strike a number of unlikely alliances.
Riding the Trinity like a sled, Vladimir Mayakovski hits the wall.
Solzenitsin, with a mountain of Christmas packages containing
millions of little concentration camps, stumbles on a
banana peel and goes straight through Carol Burnett, out her
middle.
Awkwardness awaits all members of this genre.
There is one commercial only in the entire history of the world:
God, and it only comes on once a year, at night.
In it, He says this: "Any man (mensch) with a maimed prick who
seek shelter from the snow, must first bury his axe."
Behind Him, a thousand doors open as if the piggybanks in the
Sky
are broken, and showers of gold coins come down on you.
Russia has unfastened her skirts.
There is a storm of icons, re-raging Saint Georges, feathers,
feathers, basements full of paper Stalins, hairpins,
lutes, knock knock who's there, short prayers.
Meat! Clocks! Geography! Time! All Go Boom!

THE CRUCIAL
HAS BEEN NAMED AFTER THE CROSS
THE HISSING CROSS
THE SAMOVAR

These, comrades, are teethmarks on the wall.
I made them out of boredom.
I lie in a clean bed now under the gaze
of ten faithful scribes working
on my theory of the Great Central Sorrow.
The moon shines from a whorl of blue snow.

116

Through the baroque dacha door loaded with wooden saints
comes woman on horse Alice Codrescu, and says:
I come to change your punctuation!

The Life on Film of St. Theresa

She carefully wrapped an egg in each sock
of the martyr who died of shock.
She tied them around her neck, and was wandering.
One day she bled at an inn, in the snow.
The air was pierced by arrows of Ave Maria, sudden
flurries of wings. Open the bound encyclopedia,
and let me into the brown sky, Mother of God, she cried.
A frozen woman under an icicle basked in simplicity.
The book opened: in it, the Savior was squeezed tight
'twixt Salad and Savoir. Still, there was room in Heaven.
She arrived at his side on the pinpoint of her emotions.
Two large circles of sweat danced around her shoulders.
She saw from there things big indeed, and cherished.
The snow is awake, clouds loom, wars break in print,
she cried, and I am full oh beasts called Past & Light,
of an animal love, and I see, at all times, a great
furry animal loving me, with the same passion!

Jingling the Cookery

More food! The food of anxiety! The vivacious
spiralling appetite of progressing paranoia!

The amazing bridge of sausages between mother & son!
The flat pancakes on which all the relations sit
watching ducks frying in the future
while on the river stuffed with fish, the poor man
pushes his canoe against the current which begins
in his wife's mouth!

What salad makes you and me contain so much amour?

Beans disguised as health, why do you stare
down the encompassing vistas and pile
yourselves up in little mountains on the table
to be played poker with?

The horizon is a nut, we are the advancing investigative
units of God poking our thermometers in the flour,
checking the dates for worms, and carrying
within us, a great potential for violence
like an empty burlap sack

out of which neither you nor I will emerge hungry

Getting There

The sun shakes the man while
the moon hits him
but he keeps going because he's aiming
to go to the factory and get his brain
changed.

He has a new body, he is going to ask for a new brain.

That was the sun that was, he says,
shining on the man I am not.
That was the moon that was
hitting places that don't hurt any more.

The factory is not far off if only
I can hold out by swaying in my infancy
like in an easy chair
a Gary Cooper in the tropics

If only I can save my breath
like a warm man in search of diamonds
if only I could stop.

Years later the set is the same.
He's aiming for the factory but this time
he's on a train, an armored train

The Yes Log

Say Yes to all and be condensed in fact!

Poems are sermonettes for all the interlocking
tremors in the land.

The brain turns toward its great surprise
like a revolving door holding
a giant red ant
                    Surprised?
It rains with gusto.

What are we doing here with the recipe for father?

Take two parts sand and one part ladder.
Mix with parsley, fry and scatter.

And then say Yes to the precisely knotted whip
which lashes
down your succession and up your ancestry,
so that in touching
each past or future face it can
change you from shit to gold?

O stamp of hell o electricity!

The Question of Personnel

Glorious summer day! Clump of hot rocks!
I am naked looking at the vulture heading down
for my aspirin bottle! (Vultures get
these immense headaches from so much blue)
These rocks are an anchor, else I'd be up there with you.
I would sail for an encore anywhere.
The eyes of a thousand skinny runts are focused on me.
If he can do it, they say, why can't we.
I'm not about to do it, I'm too attached to my aspirin.
It would be good to walk up to the medicine cabinet
on a fine day for the ego and say to the aspirin bottle:
Eat my ass! It's the best thing going these days!
and then firmfingered grab it by the childproof cap
and throw it to the vultures.
Ah, then I'll be up there to congratulate the father
of Creative Jive!
Lord, I would say, forgive us our hidden intentions
even if they are clear to you.
It is our clarity, I know, that baffles you.
I know that as I explain myself my state of mind rivals
that of the angels.
Then I would begin to embroider:
I have worked, Sir, on this quilt for 30 years.
I am in the middle of it and with your permission
I would like someone else to finish it.
It is this half a forest with lean unicorns
fucking each other in a grove of fir
and all my successor has to do is put
a little more love into it and a couple of soda-
fountains so that everyone will know it was made in America.
My intuition does not side with a vast burst of nonsense.
In Heaven embroidering is a dignified occupation.
The rinse in the wine glass foams in Double O Crochet
on the lips of the assemblage.
The termite is taking her siesta, the house is no more.
A faded man shines in a novel.
From the mind rises the Paragraph.
The years lift like inches of skirt above the knees
but there is barely any urgency to time.
All things it seems are grateful and fair

to the wall through which the chronometer ticks.
Hot rocks! Summer day! The girls go by
smuggling flutes into the trumpet section.
Sans vulture, the sun, where it sits, cloaked in causality,
is a Seurat of tiny monks taking their pillows to heaven.

The Differences

for Barbara Szerlip

When it comes to sentiment, as it will, you can't compete
with the bourgeoisie, or with the radio.

*

It says on my diploma: sheer irresponsibility with a
touch of cruelty: the man is licensed to practice.

*

i'm really shy
and deep
inside
i don't give anyone the eye
enter the
     nude
   bride
      descending
  the spiral
    staircase

*

On their knees, people say funny things. I always tell
them: You will speak normally, when you recover!

*

One more inch and you're out of a job!

*

If a fleeting impression is the whole performance, the fact
of something nameless enters the body of the fierce yolk,
endlessly urging the egg to scramble itself.

*

You are intelligent, my heart goes out to you.

*

The trees may be scary
but hidden among them
is your house

*

I am St. John the Baptist, my work heralds the birth of
Jesus.

★

Future delights are an attack on their sources: only miracles
are relevant.

★

You got somethin horrible
And God said that you must die
So you turn to poetry
And began to cry-eeee

★

There is economy in the unconscious. The horses of Apocalypse
are on a ration of hay. Heaven is not running out of miracles
but there are fewer Distributors.
I am offering you a job.

★

The degenerate
vampire

haunts the out-
skirts of the hemo-
philia camp

★

The man is a woman, the woman is a man, their child is
silent between them like the lights of a strange city
underlining the vast differences.

★

She lived in a bottle of Black & White, he lived in her
closet. Their children, the blackbirds, swooped down on
them in the winter, and flew away in V flocks, their feathers
staying behind as pillows, mementos.

★

The employment of difference is not a big business, the
universe looks with indifference at evolution.

★

He refused to let them cover his eyes
and as the volley began
he shouted:
vive la différence!

*

The devil's sense of humor spawned photorealism while
impressionism tended to favor god.

*

The objective observer laid his rifle on the wrong side
of generalisation, and sleep took him apart like a watch.

*

Daytime, an arbitrary variety of.

*

Degeneracy is the fruit of sympathy. Us healthy animals
we like to kick ass.

The Marriage of Insult and Injury

At first, Insult follows Injury like a choo-choo train
everywhere, into stores, into deeply grooved bodies.
Injured from within I could not wait until they come in.
So I cook something poisonous, I ring a bell.
The word is out: an injured Injun mills about the Insulting
Totem, with a palm pressed to the wound!
Injury comes first, an engine in her stride. "Cripples,"
she says, "Have taken over the gym,
and clustered in deficient lumps, they are
Insulting a Smooth Body, an uninjured, smooth, flawless,
egglike body, on which Insult trembles and falls,
like water on a duck, it falls flat on its 'Fuck!' "

That was perception before the union, back when
Uninsulted the Injury hopped forth toward the Healer,
Uninjured the Insult headed toward certain Evaporation,
And insult met Injury with a view to containment
Not bringing Baby Forth.

Then comes Insult: "The order of things
Is no lock to be tampered with.
To make a cliché budge is to bug the Universe!"

Between us, in the ordinance room, the boiler explodes.

Ahead by 6½ insults, the injuries multiply:
the cleaning crews double as juries.
Decay is musical, proof is obsolete.

I have performed a wedding *splendide, j'ai épousé la nuit.*

Undaunted, the anesthetic begs to be conjoined
with an esthetic worthy of subduing.

The Park

What is recorded
does not lack passion, standing power or suspense,
yet where does this rage spring from that mows
the people down and bleeds the cows?
If any process, any flowing thing
is really nothing,
if the night is really nothing,
where does this hysteria, this great compulsion
to witness a basic sadness,
come from?
Do I pull myself by conclusions like an elevator
or is this, simply,
boredom by the flowers?

A victim of lively interest and constant bending.

How can I close the window or the book and be
alone with the torrential
manners of my skin? How keep
the claws half-out, the icepicks half within?

If only, as I write, the words would get obscene.
If only they would stand on their long legs
and turn
their full nakedness on me
like spotlights

sucking dead birds and prisons out of darkness.

What could, without foreclosure, audits and ruins,
warm this heart and offer
completeness to the brain?

Mint, parsley, violets and dandelions?

Is there a private park around here
to know the name of and then
roll on its views?

Orbital Complexion

The technology of soul restoration
is a clever dose of miracles, insomnia, drugs,
poetry and cannibalism

How do you put an old newspaper back
on the stand? Without losing
your grasp on the technology? Without
blunting the tools, and easily,
like a warm wind?

The great surprise is in having revealed
an exact prior knowledge,

so that each one, rooted like a smiling cheese
in a storm of knives, could lift
his or her snails from the cabbage leaves
and eat the world

Xerox the Spirit and Be Well

The outside comes in
to watch itself—well, fuck it!
The inside gets out.
Goodbye.

When will I have a shiny mind?
A mind on which the balls can roll, and the trains.
A mind in which the years leave tracks for some
original suppleness to roll
out of it like trains.

Will they unearth the stations,
clean up the plains?

"They" go by silently and nothing,
nothing is smooth,
no, not when you stand sulking
inside an out-of-season marigold and paw
your reasons like an angry worm
as the floors sway, pushed by remote control
by the military.

Nothing, nothing will ever stop
because under us the soil
boils with psychotic illusions!

Space Soufflé

There is only content
pleading "no contest" to the cracked egg
of energy, lifting itself out of parents
into Paris where they are waiting
with candles and champagne

What are they waiting for while loving
the content of their hands?

The universe, which is a hero's welcome,
is merely a description
to be waited on, day and night,
with one foot always in the air

The lovers of the Air Force line the streets,
watching their loved ones fill the sky
with energy, and crashing into towers

The contents spill
so that this night won't be forgotten

Head trapped by seeds and helicopters

Old Cities

The contentment is seen at the tip. I am so
anxious to see the little light and win.
But it is tipped off by the rain, the little light,
and by the lane that ends ahead.
I should get angry but I get sad.
In other cities, at other times, the little light
was everywhere. I couldn't sit in buses
because it burned the seat. Those are, perhaps,
its cities and the buses
are where it lives.
Will they, when I return, return my light?
Or will I hit my center at the moment
I discover it gone? And in that hit I will see water.
I chase my light with buckets of black water.

For Thom Gunn

The coffin sealer is fanatical.
He can't stop nailing what he can't
understand like nailing poems
to a great directness. Stop it, I tell him,
as directly as I can, stop it, but he keeps
driving steel through all my tender inns:
The Inn of the Beginning, The Outside Inn.
I am not a coffin, I am splendid whichever
way you see me, splendid, radiant and free.
I am a splendid coffin, a page from the Bible
on which Salome lies,
all myrrhed, oiled, shiny
and so ripe for fucking that I get horny
even now, 2000 years after the fact.
It is her isn't it?
And still I stand before a rain of nails
watching depression, sorrow, disaster, fear, horror,
tightness and control.
The miracles just don't come fast enough.

Sadness Unhinged

for Dubcek

A faded man shines in a novel
like a Jew in a 1943 photo.
There are
translucent sands that nurse the step along:
Where are you going?
You I will nurse along for not remembering.
I hurt. At the back of my head, a hand
pushes the skull inward.
I have lost the sense of my life.
I am cold sober.
I see the stove and I count the bullets in the revolver.
A hand has pulled from the inside
all that made firmness firm,
the velvet without the valuable,
the gut of the balloon,
the air.
I am of an intricately flawed quality,
my gourds are singed, I will not tamper with the river.
I am a dog, lost in the dark, lonely, cold and humid cement
cell of the Humane Society,
waiting for my owners who will not come.

*

My despair like this poem
comes only once.
My terror is constant.
I live with the forked ends
of a formal victory.
I live without a tent.
I am not satisfied with ambiguity,
it takes two of them to get me off.
Duality often, out for a swim,
drowns in ambiguity.
I sustain joy in the mortality
of the hair, or the green section.
Nothing is too extreme
for my erection.
Why not, like this erection,

tend only to your own beliefs?
Imitate your cocks,
you foolish heads!
Girls, find your own metaphors.
Imitate your cocks
the heads of which light
the way; there are prisms
buried in them, diamonds cutting
their way out of museums, cubes
of light singing navels to sleep.
If you imitate well
I will let you out of Hell.
The light in Hell is sick.
The sign MOTEL flickers on and off.
Tiny bluebeards carry silver coffins
with rococo handles.

Everyone around me is dying.
But not the ones I love.
A warped sentimentality begins
to take apart the barn.
Will the cow stand the rain?
Death stalks the bushes
in Santa Barbara.
My friend JR bids me look at his gun,
a thing out of Dostoievski whom
many of you will be reading again,
and says: "With this, I'll check out."
There is no air, only endless
luggage counters in sterile terminals.
Pain racks his body and he throws
the morphine out the window
like Coleridge, and I weigh the gun, say:
"You mind waiting until
I get out of the room?
I hate a mess."
"But the world," said he,
"if that's a mess,
how can you stand it?"
The distance between realities is anyone's guess,
and what grows on it, less and less.

One kindergarten child, alone, trudges up hill carrying
a whole forest under his arm.
They gave it to him in school.
When I was a child, a faded child in an old country,
in a poor school, in a poor country,
learning was the pleasure of watching Something come out of
Nothing; not paper, certainly.
You, American kindergartner, are taking home the body
of your mother, her pubic hair. What are you going to do
when you get home, and she is not there?
Oh, child, I am so sorry. But what happened to you?
Why are you so tall, of a sudden? Why do your shoulders
have basketball hoops? Why does your tee-shirt say
HOMO AMERICANUS, in letters as large as the clouds?

A Cook in Hell

1.

As I was going whistling down the hill of Hell
I saw a man shitting through the top of his head:
there was a hole like a bell and through it came
the golden turds, and other matters dead.
Half human and half porcelain, these beings filled the sky.
Have they golden intelligence? Or are they acrobats
composing the fetid ritual of an ancient dawn? I said
to myself, upon spotting so many more, everywhere.
Priests, whores, acrobats, charmers, all convinced
by the well placed brown rose at the top of their hair,
launched their canoes into the higher air,
as uncontrolled and joyous as a barrel full of nymphs.
Sighing, I continued my descent, down the singular
lane with its peculiar beauty, of slaughtered innocents
planted like peanut trees in the black sand,
watching me with poisoned envy, turning every bend.
On this road I saw a woman trudging uphill away from
what must be the inconceivable basements of Hell,
and two children trudged after her, and a husband.
As we pass, she points a long pointed index
at the direction I am going in, relentlessly obsessed,
and says: "I like your direction better than mine"
and I'm rooted to the spot, uncomprehending, to say:
"You always can, my house is Thine!"

2.

She leaves her life and follows me, back on the road to Hell.
There is a stand along the road, a shiny, modern kitchen.
She hangs the shopping bag from a hatrack which also is a hand
that sorts meat from cheese and parsley root from pepper bell,
and sits in a rotunda, overlooking a yellow ocean self-possessed
to a metallic point, and sand dunes full of skulls marked "Sell,"
while I boil purple water in which a fetus swims or seems to jell
and chop the huge mushrooms we have called "Hats," both for
    their
size as well as for their politeness to the knife.
They are hats for very large heads these meats of which

the dirt is rife, these ancient sprouts of wisdom and these harsh
citizens of moss-filled bogs and caves and swamps,
the heads of, say, Saint Francis or Pascal, heads known
to be both large and filled with thoughts and serial complaints.
I pray, as I bring down the knife, that there are no heads inside
these hats; I pray also that in the coming night
shade will not stray from us; and finally I pray that every slice
will be noted, and recorded, not once or twice, but thrice.
But heads there are because this is the road to hell.
Au revoir, Saint Francis, I didn't meant to faint the balcony.
Their tears owe their sublimity to your pain, not my ignorance.
Adieu, Pascal, you can love your God now!
If I had not just now killed them how would they have died for
        you?
The cook must invest in pain, he will be questioned about sorrow
not happiness, or joy, or rain. He is not protected by a wall
of glass bearing the fingerprints of the working class, as are
the artichoke hearts, already torn out of the artichokes.
He is alone in a field of slaughter which he would like to close.
A hundred souls, awake, supervise his activity, and buzz.
If he yielded for a second to look these extraordinary bees
of the departed, into their sunken eyes, he would find himself
at the bottom of a valley, among twisted propellers,
he would perceive the future with a groan, a howl and a sigh,
as a continuous, hysterical, subterranean, snaky and avuncular
Revolt, spreading under the ground to the potatoes, to the lily
bulbs, to the onions, and to the carrots, rousing them
from tubercular somnolence and roasting them to vicious fury,
rocketlike, in the first fireworks on the outermost rim of Hell.
There is a blindness they approve of in the name of Homer, here.
They say, on little braille tablets nailed to maimed orphans,
that the blind feel good in a thousand obscure ways, and that
the place of the cook is to use his kitchen knife for proportion
and not for surgery because Davis Pharmaceutical is in that business,
and furthermore, that the absence of sharp cuts whets the appetite.
That is what they say, and I am keeping a blue line of restraint
when suddenly I feel a boiling in my blood as if the tent
of my entire life were just right now collapsing on some floor,
and I want to enter, with my cock, into the hollows and the creases
of each legume, animal and essence, and get past the outer shell.
To the last moment, the cook must be in readiness to bring
the last joyful asparagus in the world to a standstill with a blow

on the thinnest neck at the base of the stalk, thus closing
a fair chapter in the history of the race, and opening
the window to an age of oil, a wave of which will spell to all
that thus pass the days and still no soup.

3.

And so a time there comes when one must move, and get his bag
of trinkets, to continue the steep descent below the dreamer's pits.
All around him, there are children, playing with an extraordinary
lack of awareness of either direction, or the nearness of Hell.
The woman, as they leave the kitchen, tells him that he must
either go up, back into the light he remembers so well, or they
must part, she having no intention of any further descent, and so
the tragic part is he so readily assents and everyone is getting
new ski boots, alpinists' tools, cans of rations, and a short
lecture on the ecstatic worlds of paradise, where in the freedom
of an eternal summer, the people and the trees share every meal.
As we were going thus whistling up and away from the hill of Hell
we passed a poet, much in need of food, and air, and clothing
and a great lack of say in the affairs of a demented world,
and as we passed, my woman of a whole fortnight, she said she
        liked
his direction better than hers, and together, they began what was
a brand new journey into Hell, a fresh descent and, knowing her,
in a fortnight, a brand new thrust for health, and trees, and air.

4.

The children, as the will would have it, are outlined
like trembling geese against the patchy snow of a bright day.
Only I know this brightness to be the lit halo of a saint and not
what peasants commonly mistake for day, a halo that is a circular
searchlight encompassing the bodies of the innocent in their
attic rooms reading with flashlights dirty books, and tending
to their erections, and their guitars, and their terrains,
a halo tuned to be both not too bright and not too dim, a perfect
lamp in the immenseness of the locked-up night.
But in ascending, you must pay a toll which is to turn this halo up
in passing, as if a nightmare guides your hand, and in so doing
you will light the world with a bright cobalt blue fierceness,
waking the children in the night, making them see themselves out-

lined in blood, with their erections, and razors crossing every
game they've played like a page, scarring them forever, and so hard,
that they will always treat themselves to flight,
going from every little thing toward the safety of the night,
with pears and breasts burnt to a cinder, dancing in their eyes,
until the angels mercifully place baskets of fruit on their new graves.
All these heads framed in the harsh police light: I have
looked at all of them, Sir. The suspect is not in the line-up.
I could not turn that halo's beam on my own children so
I packed up their ropes, and tools, and back we went, toward the
depths of pure, unravaged Hell where, for the night we stopped
in the roadside kitchen, watching the poet cook a meal, for
there was now a full quire of us, and hungry, too.

5.

His kitchen had decorum, as opposed to mine which was
a mess of things, a constant urging on, and then some other things,
having to do with pity, guilt and appetite undaunted.
His kitchen was like a court lined with satin pillows: in it
one was both judged, and made love to in impromptu positions.
The cooking went on with total regard for form, and the guests
all had staple guns with which they seemed to constantly
staple posters to each others' heads, announcing that the discord
of events would be solved in a place set apart for the purpose,
during a great burst of voice, by one or the other of the present.
The children loved the din, they thought it was music, and also,
on silver screens that slid directly into their hearts, they saw
movies of their own minds going into tail-spins, or getting born,
or solving problems that then shined, and splintered like mica.
Even their sleep, in this new kitchen, was made from the substance
of a thing apart from their dreams, from the dreams of others or
from the dreams of many anguished historical nights, or unknown,
it was a sleep like that of well-fed slaves who fell into the glass
of their own image, and then budged no more,
it was the sleep of slaves fed on philosophy, and dogs fed on time,
a sleep I should have whips for, when I pass.
And yet, like in my kitchen too of not so long ago, the nights
passed like the days, and still no food, and still
the distance steadily remained the same from Hell, and the view.
And to the children then I bid goodbye, who stood there saved
from cobalt light and burning halos, who stood there fusing

with strange life-forms, octopi and horses, outlined by the decorum
of the kitchen, surrounded by small flames, and literature,
who stood there like windows behind which the unhappy
  forefathers
strained their ghostly eyes, watching for a sign.
The depths of Hell were winking and again, I started for its lights.

6.

My birth, they tell me, is a house, and my destination is a store.
A strange mother this, sending me out for more, and more.
So on the road going through the woods, from my house to the
  store,
I call myself Animal, and am ready to act like one, or two,
should love appear, in the nude, with breasts, and nipples, and
maybe a scar or two, or a limp, or a distinctive smirk, should
she appear out of nowhere, on the road through the trees through
which the town appears dimly, with flaming cupolas, and Exxon in
the night sky, should she appear now, together we might fly.
Certainly, elegance must be careful, and geometry stand up to lust.
But the trees mock me, the love I see doesn't last, there is only wind
and I am awkwardly dressed among these trees, which I feel
like cutting down, before I buy, from the store, bread, cheese,
and *Oui* magazine, and a score of unrelated complexities, for Mom.
Ah, but a pervading melancholy makes mushrooms the fashion in
  hats!
Ah, but for the mind from which rises the Paragraph!
I walk alone and I begin to slide but I am careful not to slip
on the downward slopes of Hell, on the shiny long trail with a
  prong
in Eternity, through which flows oil, and fluid materiel,
I am careful not to use the voice against itself to tell
jokes too horrible to hear, punchlines from which the laughter fell,
I'm careful, but in such a reckless way, God only knows and He is
off the air, as I walk alone through the Four Squeezes:
Squeezed between the pages of news, politics eats only raw heart.
Squeezed in the paraplegic's hook the bulb fits in the tricky socket.
It is getting worse for Jews and Americans.
Squeezed between the rise of professionalism and the mushrooming
of cheap feeding stations, the cook is fed to Madame La Mort.
Squeezed between bargains I feel that I am an opportunity
for civilization, and for what forms choose to remain when the devil

139

uncovers the pot, to see how it's cooking.
As I was going whistling down the hill of Hell
I saw that such forms were pure as chose to remain:
some flocked away when the blood slowed down,
others when the tiny umbrellas collapsed in the wet fields,
and others yet disappeared when the only razorblade in the universe
was found half-imbedded in the wrist of God, thus making it hard
to chop up the promised reward into the finest grain there is.
But others stayed to march into the flames with me, and be
consumed by both large and small fires, like criminals in joy,
skating on necessity, realized in speed, born in the heat
of a mother and father chasing each other around a lit dial.
Nothing was merely or yet human. Spring came, the ice melted,
through the holes in the clouds I saw figures and facts,
the wrong facts, the right figures, and then I saw my goal:
a pasture full of Gypsies riding their horses through the holes.
Under them, all of us were going on foot, pushing our bodies
through a huge, clean ear, through the flames of a wide ring.
I have no patience, said the President of Hell, with those
who do not pay precise attention to their present circumstances.
I can barely emphasize the danger!
And yet, all around him, extreme logic was in effect,
and yet, warmed by his voice we were jesters at the courts of
    Librium.
The master of Hell was a dinosaur on a couch, drawling out
the psychoanalysis of the paleolithic, posing for a picture by
Alice Codrescu, © 1976, and dispensing advice to the free to hear.
To the one next to me he said: "Push the furs aside,
and ask to see the Furrier!" To another, he advised: "Go find
a lawn and start a revolution among the worms!" And to me, he
    said:
"Everywhere they are boarding the buses to work."
"Sleeping securely when everyone is gone, is a luxury you do not
    have."
"Not in a thousand years, not in your grave."
"I think that you are ready to audition for the Night
and you might or you might not get a part!"
Before I could thank him, the world parted, and I was swimming
in a black river from the middle of which a rapid deep current
beckoned, and out of which a gruesome fish came and said:
"Audition in 10 minutes for all the bathers up stream!" of which
I was one. And surely, soon I drowned, with others but alone.

140

A number of them looked me over: not enough dark meat for
    the night!
Not enough protein for Hell! Back to the Day!
At this, I was forced upward suddenly, like a man in a geiser
    chair,
and I found myself climbing the slopes, away from Hell,
with a new view of things in which order was not essential
but the very next meal very much so, a new view from which, I
    must
tell, pride is missing, and only the shell of it all stays.
Of course, I stopped by the kitchen, half way up to tell
a number of café regulars of which you are one, that the director
of Hell adored me in secret, but sent me back for my friends.
When we go *en masse*, I will promise to better polish my tenses.
Until then, will art override the expenses?

Momentary Bafflement with Return Home at Dawn

Extremely logical circumstances are in effect:
we are in danger of behaving as expected (though
how to create a red rage or what anyone expects
and where ...) I feel
most strange: could someone have taught me an iron-
clad logic while I was sleeping at Carmen's house?
Oh, Christ, push the furs aside
and ask to see the Furrier! Sir, do you know
anything about this? I was coming home appalled at the
submivissness
submissiveness
of lawns and yet I could not start
a revolution among the worms. It was
strange indeed to find my madness lacking militancy.
I am not, Sir, pleased. I would like my perceptions
to march on the capital! Un-
fortunately I cannot appeal to other madmen: we
are all mad in different ways and the wonderfully
sane masses will never hear this pitch: they are
boarding the buses for work.
Everywhere they are boarding the buses to work.
The right to insist must be natural.
If they are, I will too. Sleeping securely
when everyone is gone is a luxury I do not have.
I smoke too many cigarettes for that; I think
my body is made of a soft alloy of dead cats and lead
and folded to requirements.
I wouldn't mind auditioning for the Night
just as long as I don't get a part. Just for the
experience. I have a bad memory,
it's possible that I already have. In fact,
I remember: There was this river
in the middle of which a rapid and deep hole beckoned.
Out of it a fish came out:
Audition in ten minutes! he told
a number of bathers of which I was one.
And surely, soon we drowned.
They looked me over: not enough dark meat for the Night!
Try the Day!
Ah, well, I surfaced with a new view

of things in which order was not essential,
greed even less so.
Of course, I can't be sure that secretly
the director adored me or not, I tell
a number of café regulars of which you are one,
but one never knows for sure if *mission* isn't really
an issue.
So there, have a cigarette.
In the Cavity at the heart of *this* matter
things are occurring I wouldn't to any recommend,
things both disgusting and completely eerie.
There is a law I imagine, carved on the walls the way
the Communists carve little heads of Lenin, the way
life is carved on palms for all to see,
but what this law purports to regulate is well
beyond me. The question is:
can one ask the driver midway down the precipice at the
foot of which a ten-foot spike looms, if he could
please turn around and sign here?
Or the glove out of control, inside the vagina, provoking
the race to a duel, if it would please return
to the hand it fell from when it slapped the Intruder?
Now or never, one would like to say, tomorrow
they close the post offices.
Yes, but we will still have bath-
rooms and handcuffs! Chairs and gladiolas!
A different species inhabits the laboratories!
The joy is so great one would like to shout goodbye to
every one of one's sperms: 20,000,000,000 goodbyes!
Goodbye, goodbye, goodbye!
Once in a while one makes it to my eyes.
I couldn't make it in the outside world, honest.
The space would render me catatonic, soon they would
have to pack me against the wall under a lantern
with a bunch of souls sad indeed.
I'm getting off the bus: they have something missing
in their gait, they have
women propping them up everywhere, lighting matches
after orgasms.

The Penal Cavalry

QUIT PLAYING GAMES!
START FACING THINGS!
and then i stopped playing games
and i faced things
and all i could think of was
I WOULD LIKE TO WRITE A BOOK CALLED
"THE PENAL CAVALRY"
and this book was from the point of view
of someone who faced things
and this someone found that he couldn't
leave his room because each thing
he faced had a thousand faces
and staring into each one in turn
took a very long time
so one day he joined
THE PENAL CAVALRY
which was a way of facing things
at a fantastic speed
on top of a horse
and he found that facing things
this way
he could have
a little time for himself
a time in which he closed himself up like a shell
and faced nothing
for hours on end

The Monk

I saw a fantastic description of a monk's cell. This monk made wine and one wall was lined with barrels and bottles while another held a wide bookshelf. In the middle was a solid oak table on which there was a lamp and a variety of papers. The cell was in the woods and the woods were in the mountains on a gentle slope facing East. Everything the monk wrote he read to the trees and in the fall, when he made his wine, he poured some of it on their roots from big clay jugs. Every time I feel depressed I think about that monk and how, as long as there are trees, I can be just like him and then nothing depresses me any more.

In the Supermarket

What are these objects everyone speaks of? Why is it that not one day can pass without mention of forks and clothes? The other day, in a supermarket, I started to cry. Only instead of tears I was secreting a band of small black eggs which immediately broke and released thin black birds. Everyone looked up from the shelves in which in which they had been engrossed reading the labels and congratulated me at the top of their voices. I didn't know what to say so I tried crying again to please them but this time no tears came. I was left to do my shopping alone and a great sadness tore at my innards without an inkling of where it came from and why it made everything seem so worthless.

The Lady Painter

She is painting an eye on the side of a hill. We watch her through binoculars but she has already painted the ends of our binoculars black. She goes on painting over an eye here and then painting an eye over the eye she painted over. This way she is always looked upon, stared at and anxiously avoided with a sideways glance. It makes no difference. She is the soul of chance, this is what it says on her tee-shirt: THE SOUL OF CHANCE.

Center Piece

I can't think of any man or woman without also thinking "poor man!" "poor woman!" This "poor" is a box I've created over the years. There is nothing inside it and this is precisely why it is my favorite creation. Even the walls of this box are made of nothing. I love to contemplate when night falls, this box made of absolutely nothing with nothing inside, just sitting there in the middle of myself surrounded by so many things and by so much anxiety. It is always quiet when I become aware of it and if it wasn't for the fact of my mortal body I would enlarge it to contain the Universe.

Toward the End of 1969

suddenly toward the end of 1969 everything is
"objectified" after a fashion that leaves
you in your clothes but not in your mind
and every day sees
the birth of new instruments, wooden and
metallic, born out of circumstance, conjecture
and plain absence. not to under-
estimate these things a new set of values
is also born and not only one does not under-
estimate but one praises
lavishly, completely, with the dedication
of a saint to the cross. sets of
paternal and maternal perception knock
patiently at the doors of the brand new cubicles
like infant birds in eggs with a right
to this world but, really, what right
to my world does a cane, a shoe or a hat have
what right except part-time presence?
i wonder but it all comes to this: even i
see no wrong with the 90 per cent "alien-
ness" of the world and i
should know better because i
am a poet

Tetrachlorine

The termite is taking her siesta, the house is no more;
the rinse in the wine glass foams in Double O Crochet
on the lower lip of the assemblage;
the dishes are filled with ham; the wind farts;
from the mind rises the Paragraph;
the years lift like inches of skirt above the knee
giving a certain urgency to time; the young hopeful
strives on in his haste to meet the young fool.
Thus all things are grateful and fair
to the wall through which the chronometer ticks.
Smuggled into the trumpet section, the flute makes her bid.
The fog where it sits, cloaked in causality, looks
like a Seurat of tiny monks taking their pillows to heaven.
I am an opportunity for civilization, a bargain.
The light fits into the tricky socket.
To this light this mind flocks.
Roll up that dress, slowly in the lit (barely)
window of the castle throwing candle-
light on my binoculars. We have just stepped from the gas-lamps
away from the opera glasses, it is
another century and we are undecided. Roll it up,
at your pace, in the harsh neon of fifty
or a hundred years later, roll it up slowly or roll
it away, roll it in such a way that we might
enter the next century simultaneously atomic
and cunt-struck. Stun us with your coquetry!

A myth to have to curl around at night
to pluck (delicately) at the emerging pubis
with the pincers of one's star,
never once failing in mid-sentence or tumbling
off the bed into the waiting pit.

But one must bear the sight of one's hand, day
and night, night after night. One must sit in the wet
puddle of this fog and draw checks from the Source!
Having become the hero of one's own misunderstanding
of the world, one must not tarry but,
steeped in legend, he must now take one of the available
observation posts and relieve the guard.

Au Bout du Temps

So late in the 20th Century
    So late in the 20th Century
    At the end almost of the 20th Century
I sit in my home
    In my modest and meaningless home
    And worry about my penis
    ABOUT MY PENIS FOR CHRISSAKES!

In praise of biology
    In praise of visions . . .
Only a few years ago it did not seem
    so late in the 20th Century
    it did not seem very late
        in the 20th Century
    this saddest of centuries
maybe the 14th was a very sad century
    fin de siècle
        mal de siècle
mal de fin
    so late in the night
    so late in the century
    in the 20th Century

Honesty can't be encouraged in individuals. It must be a conclusion of effort. It is easier to be honest. The mind is a squashed banana after a lie. Out of this squashed banana there often rises the energy of genius but look what syphilis does to it. It is not guilt squashes the banana but the wider perspective, the cosmic connections. The mere need of connections is a first step of the boot on the banana. That we should have a banana for a brain testifies to its youth. Diamond brains can lie all they want.

149

Selavie

Why is it so hard to start exactly where I'm at?
Not yesterday in the refuse or tomorrow in Italy
but from the puff of smoke curling over the blue
of my manly Smith Corona 220, a smoke signal
to my mother for her to send new clippings about cancer
from *Reader's Digest, The Washington Post* and the
National Geographic. Everywhere someone is defending
a piece of the picturesque. Maybe there isn't
anything to start with but that's absurd since every second
the dough rises and the bell is about to ring.
A mad black dog will walk through the door.
A howling will begin in the red telephone.
The posters will fall from the wall. The working class
might be rising. Night might fall. Wind may blow. Rain may
drench us to the bone and cold may eat our noses.
And yet, the American way is to keep working.
Sombitches these Americans, father dies, brother drowns,
wife runs away but the logs must go down the river.
The trucks are waiting and the goods must move.

Stock Report

Nobody speaks of it but destiny is currency today
and the new market is the human psyche
vaster than continents much grander than geography.
Today's capitalists look within.
From the quirks of your free flights hang the products of tomorrow!
As for me, Sir, I don't have any feelings. I just have gods.
Right now I am the favorite of Depression, a mean and petty
                    god with dirty fingers.
Yesterday I happened to tangle with Love, by the river.
When the people have no more feelings
the gods turn to each other for company and stagger the world
with imaginative pageants, slaughters, miracles and ruins.
Tomorrow's man will be a voyeur wishing for night
under the faucet of stars too bright for sleep.
Get hold if you can of a little room all black buried in a
velvet bale under the ground without windows
and return the valve from where it was removed.
We must be absolutely without importance
until we regain our advantages.
Then one day we will stage a magnificent revolt.

A Good Thing When I See One

Good thing I'm in a dark room eating rocks.
I could be in the light stroking the lizard on my arm.
If it takes
the government, the police, the publishers, the spiders
and whoever else is after me—and if they aren't
why I talk is beyond me—for a decent sacrifice
I will certainly rip their guts with my own Swiss army knife.
Now those are old offerings and perhaps
only my heart will do
or my brain or my lungs or my feet or my eyes
maybe I should be a nazi crushing the fingers of my piano hand!
It takes a lot. It takes a lot of nerve. It takes me by surprise.
It takes all it can get. It takes the getting. It takes
the getting up. It takes my wallet, my watch and my keys.
It takes friends. It takes friends by the throat. It takes
the cultivation of reality. It takes reality. It gives
reality. It takes reality. It gives reality.

À Francis Ponge

Unlike virtue
style doesn't require any examples. Examples can use
the extra time to acquire style. They could mount
a campaign against being called Examples. They could
be Events. We don't want to be examples. We just want
to happen. Where will the police be without examples?
Where the professor? Where the state? Where the censor?

Drowning Another Peasant Inquisition

Jealousy runs only skin deep.
Underneath lies the joy of not possessing.
Thus spoke the sage caressing
his one and only claim to love

as all were seated, thinking.

Between friends silence is your best bet,
he continued.
O oneness of bodies firmly planted breasts
and proudly set cocks

as on the streets, the rest
are pulled along by long streaks of bad luck

of which we know the reason.
The many windows framed in yellow light
are pulled together making
mind structures, more mind chains
around the masses, falling through the season.

One day to see
One day you will be free

That day you come and see me
That day you see me, hear

"MAN" and "WOMAN," these are horrid words, they annoy me. They chase me through the world these two, hunting my spirit with a damp blanket of grim assumptions. "MAN" is a load of perilous experience hardening inside something called "MATUR-ITY" like a boiled hotdog in an inflating blanket of dough or a limp air mattress into which a frantic tourist blows his lungs as the ship burns, and "WOMAN" is somebody who will look through every one of my gestures with a gaze loaded with sandpaper and after making me entirely transparent put her boot through the glass. I much prefer boys and girls. I much prefer girls and boy. I much prefer innocence. I much prefer blind love and joy.

Sunday Sermon

All sound is religion.
Language is merely a choirboy in this religion.
Sometimes a bishop wind rattles the windows.
Still, I must speak the most intelligent language available
while I have this typewriter knowing full well that tomorrow
I might be able to welcome a color Xerox machine into my
        studio
and with it there will be a revolution in my life.
And this revolution will wipe out the need for words.
I will say nothing for a few years to prepare for a new
revolution. Revolution. The word is like a revolver on a
sunlit window sill. It is one of the few words that sets
my heart on fire. Girl also sets my heart on fire.
Girl & Revolution. Revolution & Girl.
I am twelve years old and I intend to stay that way.

It takes joy to listen and it is inspiring being listened to. People who half-listen are half-inspiring. But I will go half and half with you if we fuck too. Fucking makes up in intensity the half that isn't listening. And it makes up the unlistened half too. In fact, we will fuck in the cemetery where no one is listening and no one is listened to. Listen to me. I will listen to you.

Matinée

A man must not be engaged if he is to float to the moon.
A man must not be engaged if he is not to be bored.
A man must not be engaged except in the pursuit of shock
and upon engagement, he must announce to the world that
he has just disengaged himself, and is now ready to proceed
to the next booth and ask for a commitment.
Thus falsely registered to vote he can ride out his engagement
and be subtly underpaid, but happy.
Lying on his porch in the sun with the avocados and birds
he can run thru himself on a field of inverted commas.
Unfortunately there are people pulling into the driveway
to ask for proof. His naked body proves nothing although
an engaged body is lean and nervous and a disengaged one is fat
and porous, and he doesn't look disengaged, so further
proof is in order: the field must be mowed and the self must
be full of the English language.
Good morning, world

Ode to Laryngitis

With the collapse of the vocal chords and through
the graces of laryngitis, a new perception of reality
knocked me off my divan and twisting my arms
delivered me dripping at the gates of heaven.
Where it entered my eyes, my brain, my hands
and left me speechless with occult new beauty.
The cracked voice in this throat is mine
and the oddly shaped vowels coming out of it are
the remains of the writing voice talking about
the speaking voice, the remains also of a mellifluous
bowing to bourgeois use of speech which English,
in its ever expanding luminous wisdom, has set
right on the surface for easier notice and faster disposal.
Remains, remains, and then: a pure vowel. And another.

Fascination

People pass under my windows deeply absorbed in garter belts
but they have not come for me. I tower here above their red
lit brains, whipped by the sandpaper wind that blows the skin
off lovers' wrists, not by a piece of the action. A leaflet
too blows by. A long read, a short story.

One day there is a party for the whole galaxy
and the ghost weeping for his lips remembers his lines.
The horse looks at himself in the water and sees a black
        harmonica.
The melancholy robot dances in the black box.
One day the profound evil is deprived of its music
and stripped both of its profundity and its intense satisfaction.

With a great heave the tree of my life topples
to give way to shiny rails.
I am exhaled, squeezed tight, pressed on and loved.

Ballad of the Typist

Wet skeletons play wet harmonicas in the electric
typewriter, to drive the typist mad who would rather be out,
in fine weather, not in with his Personality.
But he remembers all the beds in his life,
some made neatly, some unmade, some made of earth,
some made of blood, some made of books, and all
the bodies floating over them:
bits of himself stick out of everyone like broken arrows.
It appears now that the whole race is practicing karate
to eliminate the weather and keep him in:
Italians walk slapping each other's backs toward the Future,
Romanians with balled fists punch holes through the Scarecrow,
Hungarians pinch the half moons of each other's asses and Giggle,
at the end of piers French men & woman kiss incessantly in the
      Rain
under tanks oily Russians hug each other attempting to Turn
      Over,
in neon lit rooms Americans shake with one hand in their
      Pockets.
The Chinese would rather bow.
Armies go, leaving their exhibitionists behind.
God gives you tongue, the devil gives you hands,
the eyes are of an even stranger make.
The typing finger alone, ponders the unmade.

Epitaph (2)

He was a young guy with surrealist connections.
This tombstone does not lie
it merely stands imbedded in the sweet dark stew
waiting for the connoisseur

Election

Luminosity is an issue
perhaps a platform.
This is my love song
to the owl.
I enter the closet at dawn
to follow the funeral of a century.
It is a question of going back
to the house without doors

Blues for Casanova

The room was filled with black boxes.
There were no children anywhere.
There were six of us stuffing red gloves
and black stockings inside.

Then Daddy came in and said:
Clean up your room. The King is coming
for dinner.

The King enjoyed very much pulling
things out of black boxes.
He called this "dinner."

When the Revolution comes no one
will do this any longer.
There will be no more grace left.

Still Life

At the end of the street stands
a little green house called
PRIVATE HELL.

The young woman in the window is
giving piano lessons to a giant
flower in a smashed
flower pot

and, across the street, in the Chinese
grocery store,
the tiny chinaman arranges
roots, powders and cans in patterns
defying description

as, suddenly, the girl kicks
her legs in the air and turns
her face so that we can see her
and she's surprised and gentle and there is
light in her, she is in love

At Home

Small crimes, like pepper, make things
taste better.
Only very exotic people can commit large crimes
and not burn their mouths.
Spices, like crimes, are based
on various transgressions of the laws,
natural or social, so that
the feast, when it begins,
will cure the cells of definition.
Oh, what dishes won't we have,
says mother seeing
the world, that sudden
bite of food, that sudden shutting of a thousand
mouths on a thousand nipples.
Oh we shall have it all and then
we shall sleep

The Love of a Coat

It has been uppermost in my mind to write about my clothes
which are not much as clothes go but do their job in a suitable
manner. I have two shirts one red one purple which I never wear
and a great many tee-shirts which look much better on my wife
with her nipples rippling the cloth through the cloth I should say.
The same is true about my two pair of bluejeans which have been
ageing separately but gracefully around both of our asses. The coat
which loves me the most is a French paratrooper's army jacket
and I could tell of this love by the way in which it still looks good
after its pockets are filled with various stolen books, steaks and
loose change. The other coats love me less but, no matter, I brave
the rain & wind in them. In addition to these vestments there are
the silk and velvet things all embroidered with gold & silver
which sit on the bottom of secret closets waiting for a great day.
This day is getting closer and closer and I can tell by the desper-
ation in the love of my daily getup that the day to give up my
familiar self is looking through the windows already.

161

Don't Wait for Me

People wait for their mail, dogs wait for their can,
farmers wait for rain, everybody waits for death,
everybody but me. I'm not waiting for nuttin.
I would imagine I would sit down to commit suicide.
It takes a lot of nerve to commit suicide standing up.
But being in a doghouse while childhood
sprinkles sand on my ass is better than either position.
The fact is, other people are waiting for me
to tell them all this,
they are waiting to see me lay my white wrist on the VegeoMatic.
I disappoint them.
I'm a mean Motherfucker.

The Goldrush

I paint my nails gold.
My face, I also paint gold.
My body is gold already.
These gold shoes are from Provence.
Cock, solid gold.
My voice, a gold frog leaping on a gold rug.
My eyes only notice gold while I
naturally only touch gold.
In order to afford all this I work
in a pitch dark basement with a fellow I have
never seen.
Things, you know, have a golden glow.

Muffled by a Belt Across the Mouth

Words are really tiny.
The mouth is much bigger. It can take
two hundred million words to close a mouth.
Even then someone would
hang a sign on it which says OPEN
like the diner across the street which is
always closed.
Maybe we die with a mouth full of words.
Maybe this is why the dead speak
mainly to unassuming folks who never
talk unless asked.
Things being as they are, I do not trust the grave.
Be quiet, love.

End Games

To get it all back and then to notice
the use in it—what fate!
In the fields where they race motorcycles
the grass is late. In places
where the use is greater it doesn't dream
that it is used. O people
run over by tanks, you are
so blind that when you get it back
you do not think it's yours.
I want to be like you but I can't.
I've made myself so small the ants can't find me,
not to speak of weather.
I have severed my connections
before the junction. I have completed
the map so I could drive only to my center.
And there it's all together
clothed in use, and greater.

Against Meaning

Everything I do is against meaning.
This is partly deliberate, mostly spontaneous.
Wherever I am I think I'm somewhere else.
This is partly to confuse the police, mostly to
avoid myself es-
pecially when I have to confirm
the obvious which always
sits on a little table and draws a lot
of attention to itself.
So much so that no one sees the chairs
and the girl sitting on one of them.
With the obvious one is always at the movies.
The other obvious which the loud obvious
conceals
is not obvious enough to merit a
surrender of the will.
But through a little hole in the boring report
God watches us faking it.

The Threat

I am not looking for your jugular.
Only for your eyes.

That isn't exactly accurate.
I want both. And if you ask, as you should
if you like yourself, why do I go for such
ferocious treats, I must
admit

that there is something unexploded in my gut.

And it wants you because there is
an unexploded something in yours too.

A music box we swallowed when we were children?
The growing up? Which is
learning to handle terror?
Was there something in the food or is
the government responsible for it?

It's nothing I can stick my knife into and say:
"For sure it's this!"

And yet I want it out more than I want these words

À Face

I have been altered like a suit
to accommodate a much larger man.
Dedication & appalling motives support this enlargement
like crossbeams in a simple church in Transylvania.
I have gone against nature
and now I have fur.
I am the most ruthlessly hunted
but the most ecologically abundant animal.
My name is victory over mother and father.

Ode to Curiosity

It isn't just spying that turns me on.
It's also the spyglass for having
so much light as to have no memory
though it retains the feeling.
Truly, there is no perfect opaqueness in nature.
Someone is looking through me at you just as
through you
someone is staring at me.
Ah, to be a beautiful narcissist wrapped
like Christmas paper around
a gentle voyeur!
This is what I want, Seigneur!
And then to glide out of focus

Near Sonnet

I carry in my wallet the replica, cast in shell,
of Maria's clitoris.
Others have pictures in their wallets.
Adieu, flat surfaces. From now on I will carry sculptures.
When shipwrecked on the reefs of love
you find yourself hallucinating the light-house signal
coming from the tip of your cock, take thee off thine feet
and search the rocks for a totemic shape

Wishes

I wish I could appear at will in your thoughts
the way money rises into consciousness
without warning
though with dire consequences

Wishing is a body organized around
the crystal of a need
to fly

To fly with the ease of a daydream
into your solar plexus
is my contribution to the continuous
opening of your form

A watermelon in a field of lilies

I wish there was a way for many of these
futures to be known
by something other than their names

By the need for them perhaps or
by their light

The Work & the Labor

let's taste the trees, said chief
they taste like sweat, chief! the branches
of these trees are plowing the blind maps
of my classic form!! you do not like work, hmmm?
i love her, chief, the great work as *i* call *her!*
some are less patient than others though
because a glass breaks and her arm leaves the back
of the blue sofa for the black sea
on the new carpet and the island
of her sex is rising—the trees, the trees!
the whole continents of her young brain are waiting
with batons in their hands to conduct
the pores in my skin toward
those tiny filaments of glass the stars are pushing
into the leaves!   good-bye, chief,
hello, great work!   i push myself
off the ledge of birth into light

The West Is the Best and the Future Is Near

A long gold nail from the Goldrush
nails shut the box inside of which
California squirms with unbearable visions
of the Future
I am looking for my face in the Future like a straw
plowing the cocktail for another cherry
Is Anybody There? Am I there in my
moonbeam jacket crossing the street against the light
to take another look at you? And the light yet
trails the unweary detective into the trains
where the Sea swells
Perhaps my face is the horizon in the crack
between the worlds like the clouds
in Alice's pictures of sunsets

Love & the Documents

your cat disguise makes me scream   i suspect
it's no disguise at all insofar as the disguised
public officials stamping travel documents are
seeing no cat   it's not for them you're disguised tho
it's for me   and i'm disguised as "nothing at all"
which is what you are disguised as when you deal
with the law   cats, yes, have a strong will to live
even when drowned in coffee or left
swinging from the necks of tulips in the vast
garbage dumps around the city or stamped into passports
like your hair on my chest   fall gently over
the landscape like a hood, my love!   the state
of the state is solid & our state   of grace
oversees the differences

The New Gazette

I want to be the publisher of a vicious illuminated newspaper.
All the viciousness in it will be gold-leafed, raised and colored-in
by art students with medieval bodies.
The bend of their heads and the angle of their breasts
will outlast sunset
to exchange body with Chartres.
My writers will hate everything
with passion, fervor and murderous disregard for their safety
which will take in writing the form of classical tragedy.
Sophocles will be movie reviewer, Richard Speck desk editor.
Euripides and Charles Manson will be in charge of the clergy.
The translators under penalty of death will have to be faithful.
In the office only foreign languages will be spoken.
Faithfulness and alienness will be the order of the day and night
since they will succeed each other on the front page.
The paper will appear twice a day, four times at night.
The readers will be mean, nervous and ready to kill for the cause.
There will be plenty of causes, one for every hour, and in later
issues, one for every minute.
The causes will be biological and spiritual and they will incite
war for molecular differences.
Molecular terrorists in hiding will write letters to the editor.
Two persons, a man and a woman, called Tolerance and
    Intolerance,
will be in charge of love and lights.

The Discovery of Prayer

A bird
perched on a swordlike branch throws me the key
to my head which is full of sound
which presently opens and floods the place with light
for the cameraman to move in.
And whoever he is, he does.
Will we ever see the beautiful movie?
Soon the bird will go to sleep and the law
of my body
will drag my head along to a place with a ceiling
leaving the trees to find another light
for the endless documentary   Forests
of the world, march on us with the great cinema
we need to keep our souls in!

Staying with It

They used to say "deeper" and now we say "higher"

The architecture of corners versus
the architecture of circles

The neurosis of time as a mechanism in the re-
adjustment of body rhythms to cosmic music

The conversion of time into space, of matter
into energy

My life freed of memory

My poetry freed of description

All these and more
done over in Love, the color of unity

Night of a Faun

i am a peaceful mastodon at rest! clump! clump!
rat meat on the dinner table! night in moa moa!
I feel good!   the painter
who is painting us has fallen asleep! his colors
are escaping through holes in the sky on the backs
of his huge nylon brushes! why should anyone bother
with a portrait of us when the clouds have
much better faces? and much less time too!
full stomach in the center of a well loved body!
black sea! stars in the water!

The Gambling Phoenix

In minds emptied of memory like mine, no myth is lost.
Cloaked in causality, myths rage on and on, wiping out the facts.
They are a constant opportunity for civilization, an enduring
wind of particles, a never-ending renewal of rage and hope,
a cross-sexual mixture of light systems, train signals and music.
I mention music because it is raining,
a long study. It is raining a long study: at dawn
I will lift my head to the sentence to ask her "where is
your kindness now?"
All night stars poured out of my eminently sane head.
When they hit the floor, they rose to the ceiling.
When they hit the ceiling, they made a hole in it and reached the
    sky.

I reach for the standing mystery.
Lie down with me, love.

Irony as Nursery

"The inspired evil and the uninspired good,"
said the table set for two,
"are dining inside you"   Flying creatures
filled with transcendental irony like crême
de menthe flit by.   I am again, naturally
talking to myself in the manner
of a small saloon. The body is a small saloon
doing all the talking to the creature in my head
which is a spider.   While the heart
continues to be a miracle and the scenario
of the face rages publicly.   And then to think,
miserably, over a cup of coffee, how the map
is all dots of jailed men hanging
from bare electric bulbs in underground prisons
swaying between light as we see it
and the wall of light in the dark.
And when thought out all the way and seen
from all the angles, the joy of its presence, the joy of
its constancy

Working for Profit

i grow   not old   not tall   smiling
at the unserviceable idea of self
which is not my self   to which my self
serves as a tool for undoing the locks on the mysterious
language capsules whose timers are ticking
in the drawers of the state   a self of enclosure
a fossil dreaming of becoming the animal it once was
by employing me to recreate every detail
of its destroyed world   & smiling because
i am not recreating   i am playing in the mud
with a new body

Piano & Everything Nice

though many people still play the piano it's not
the piano i know.   translated in language
the black has become white not from an added
sense of irony but by an inevitable shift
at the organic level.   little girls in white
have become women in the nude.   they eat apples
but they prefer mangoes.   not from an added
sense of luxury but because of a message, a merging
between the fingers and the tongue.   at the receiving
point, the ears still bathe in music
but the key is in space like a kiss

Model Work

I model myself after someone I made up at ten walking
the mazes of my medieval city's streets, a being
so light, so bright, so fast, so generous and so complete
he almost had no body, only a black hat. Furthermore
he appeared only in the rain. To this day
he cannot be mauled because he is both outside & in.
When I think of him I feel the sorrow of my later models.
The word was a worthy model once when I had a typewriter.
Modelling is a warm march through grace without recourse.
Only the loveliest and strongest models run the course.
There is a rush to model and new models are proposed.
But there isn't a country where there are no models.
There is no rock that will not model, or sand or fruit.

The shadow in my blood will model for a fee.
And yet a lake of absent possibilities has risen
to the chin of the folk, and the waters keep rising
for what could be a model drowning.
I conversed with the drownees. What they said
turned my love for myself into syllables.
Will I be a model for my son or only endless buzzing?

Remembrance of My Forgotten Skinniness

I was a man so skinny light travelled with a
horrendous thump upward through my only vein
which the folks, naturally alert, would point
out to each other at night as I stalked
the mains of natural gas.
Often mistaken for a street lamp I would suffer
the gold urine of the ruined bums.
All this time I was nothing. I had no purpose.
A hack doctor polishing with spit a scalpel.
A wall in a church where they've buried a tractor.
I was a man so skinny I stuck to paper
and screamed at the letters.
The lettuce of desire dragged me down.
The weight of the podium could be measured in hogs.
In the bags themselves I wouldn't fit.
But when I came to America the situation changed.
Today I am a solid bank of meat.
I have just eaten critter.

Moss

A man dreams a great dream. In his dream he is covered with moss like an old tree and everywhere he looks there is a cover of moss as thick as his belly. There is moss on the binoculars and on the stars. When he awakens he goes to the door and locks it. How warm death is, he thinks. How warm and how kind! Then he pulls down the blinds and kneeling next to the refrigerator he makes delighted sounds in a muffled and distant language. It sounds as if his mouth was filled with moss.

A Still

I do not move my hands any longer. I do not
shift my legs, my eyes look straight ahead, I confine
my delirium to my blood, I have,
like Monsieur Teste, killed my puppet
with the calm in my mind.
I have struck a blow into the center where
the racial and the personal puppet
balanced each other like clowns on a tightrope which is
what happens when a continent has just been discovered
and the discoverers are having the time of their lives
stretching their language to fit the chill.
Oh the spectacle of thousands of naked owners
in private fields of blood
killing their puppets with their bare legs
like diseased chickens
and then owning nothing, finally.
This is a Discovery which lies in the Future.
Walt Whitman, who reclines in the Future
is readying the house for the party

Invitation to a Molecular Feast

I'm in a state of translation like a pregnant
animal hiding in the bushes after the passing train
The Presence of a Code
In the caves on the hill naked Laguna Beach Indians
cover up large stones with wet palm leaves
and thus, thanks to the gods who speak in several
languages at once, my eyes are also covered
and my gaze is focused on the deep black square
within me! The black gauze of geography
stretches from Red Square to the Red Sea
in the perfect night!
My Hands like Studio Lights shine over the noises
in the throats of rats gathered for the feast
I Can Sense Everything
With the bat's sense of direction with the instruction
of metals under continents
The exotic violence of a night in Paradise!

A Human Touch Misunderstood

The Cat was observing the Rule of Silence.
I touched him and he bit me.

The Stone was observing a Fast.
I sat on it and I was burnt.

My Trousers were in a Dream.
The zipper zapped me.

They are forgetting me everywhere
60 years ago I was a published poet.

Drizzle off the Ocean

The power death has   of touching   The hard
knock that knocks you in not down
into a jagged bird nest through which the feathers
of the soul squeeze out leaving a bubble of heat
and a body on the floor
                   The endless
piano practice halted abruptly by the
consciousness of another instrument
which my father never played because I would recognize it
which I will never play because I *hear* it
The room lit up by Something & seeing
lime green mammals with fur standing up on their bellies!
The light drizzle off the Ocean &
Seeing how Seeing is equivalent of something without
description with a deep aura
Oh how to be human and pretend not to be   These are
basic rights without
being forced to eat the world and how these rights finally
after eating the world
become the rights of someone else   A nameless
Someone with a point of light

Pastoral

Autumn blows a withered hand on
the velvet table to make us raise
our heads, without touching them.
Andrei Codrescu, age 65, is beyond
taking an interest in it.
He holds three aces and is going
to die in fifteen minutes.
Furious gales rip over the tall
mountains, their ends held
fast, the whip in the hand of a fat
Chinese poet on his way to an ethereal
mysterious archway over his head.
His clothes are torn
steam rises under him from the jade pool
shredding his reflection.
Inside the red gates
meat and wine rise to warm lips.

Snail Sail

The beauty is in what shocks me least.
It's in what comes without effort.
This far the only way to understand a thing
is to make it over. This is like
pounding a noodle in the door with a wet gourd.
Finding my beauty through my ego
is like that. The midgets ate the missing chord.
They will eat the whole thing, these midgets,
if you let them. There is, of course,
a way to lose it all.
To make yourself delicious and small.

Paper on Humor

Everything sounds funny in a funny magazine.
For years now I have published my poems in funny magazines
so that nobody would notice
how sad they were.
Sad anthologists, however, took my poems out of context
and put them in the sad anthologies and there
they started to shine with tears because
they were the saddest poems in there.
With a liking for funnies
and a following of sadness followers
I arrive in Brazil to get my prize.
The prize consists of the cross, the guillotine
and the hot pepper.
I am collected. Nothing matters to me.

Baltimore
1980–1981

Ethnic Jammies

an IMMIGRATION IMITATION for
those named therein

The takeover
of America
thru the 2nd person (You)
by polite men from other countries
pretending to be nude while clothed
in ill fitting suits
continues

Garlic   men
          locked
in   a   bible

Goat women
          inside
Mrs. Thwack

several of each
     fog
          over bridge

Anselm
          maneuvering the rapids
     on a tiny raft
          of quotation marks:
"Horses are just big rabbits"
          thereby detaching   THUD!
a large chunk of classical folklore

investments
     buy songs for the future
          like Mr. P. McCartney who has
just bought the rights for now
          & in perpetuity
     to
          Buddy, can you spare a dime?

Rodger

riding thru the desert
  in the sauna:
  The body is thine
  the soul is thine
  Have mercy on your woodwork
    the stock pyramid

Mr. JC
  hunting Romanoff eggs
  riding over the roofs
with the lines of high tension pasta in
  The American Night

To know
  what it can do for you
  read the side effects
    euphoria

The fractional
    people
  rise from the figures
  2.3 per TV set   clustered around
    ready to make
  the 1.4 baby of the house
    where they live
4.8 of the Life

Heat men
  composed
of garlic
    rise in a bulbous fist
from the human garden
    on The Avenue

Nanos
    discoverer of a cure
  for arthritis of the milieu
points to the sky:
        "this house
had no view before the earthquake"

Munificent muniverses

posing at Momexxon
        (last chance for a hot meal)
for Kodak (in color)

Everyone's heart
        sinks
                simultaneously

Genetic lettrists
        engineering
                the written painted city

.

The Operations of Desire

The Mailbox Whore   San Francisco 1970
The Tree-Cum-Child   Baltimore 1979
The Ice Cream Truck Telephone Call   Baltimore 1979
The News Stand Lesbians   New York 1967
The Cream Colored Public Telephone Orgy
                                    San Francisco 1976
The Half Eaten Sandwich Breasts   Monte Rio 1974
The Lamp Post Child Whore   Paris 1978
The General Hospital Supply Cafe   Baltimore 1979
The Gutter Stream Party Music And Party   New York 1968
The Manhole Steam Dancing Nude Nun   New York 1968
The Abandoned Shoes One Full Of Money One Full of Dope
                                    New York 1969
The Paperbag (Rumpled) Fortune   Then & Now
The Squashed Hat Box Cocaine Stash   Then & Now

These things and others occurred and occur.
It is to them I owe my present ability
to eroticize the world.
Bring your old things, I'll change them into objects of desire.
At first, this lab in my head was small and clumsy.
Today it is vaulted, musical and its own source of energy.
In the old days I would change a fire hydrant
into buttocks
for bread & cheese.
Today I don't eat and am working
on transforming the city of Baltimore,
a project that will take no longer than this
communique. I'm bringing
out the sexy lights, softening it here and there
around the slums (from North Avenue
to Johns Hopkins Hospital and East to Patterson Park)

When I am done
I will take on the proletariat
which inhabits the city.
Eroticize the proletariat.
Workers of the World, Disperse.
This is no mere matter of changing objects
into other objects.

188

This is being a telephone exchange allowing
the eros in people to speak to the eros in things.
The organic and the inorganic,
they make beautiful music together.
Just intercepted some gelatin
going from a busty brunette to a gay blond:
a traffic light and a yellow Camaro,
he a victim of army barbers, she a skylab hardhat.
They will presently become unquestionable humans
incontestable humans incon-
trovertible humans undoubted humans
everybodys humans
every womans human every mans woman
and others.
They is another as sure as the disturbed suburbs.
Wind in his sails, waves in her permanent.
Eppur si muove.

Traffic

At intersections
molecular desiring machines
adjusted automatically
to ulp hmmm ammm shake the fruit from youth
ah ah wait for you...
       Take it easy
           flex bolt in inner thigh
          fold wings on nipples
shed & retrieve identity
firm & wobble step
remove porcine mug
insert kosher face.
When the light changes
hobble into the arms of your love
with that look of
I hate tomorrow it was a cut up of yesterday
I'm ready for pushups
& ripe for the grave.
Cross the street saying Really really
really really really really
with a rattle a tin tied to your tail
of dog cat and man.
       Walk right over
       the industrial ruin.
Hold out your hand:
       Ah, future! In ruins before we even meet!
Point to your body
          shake head
              smile say:
Between that ruin and this ruin...ah...no deal.
          Walk faster
Light changes to
          the dawn of capitalism.
Heiresses in auto cars throw themselves
          under the wheels.
Space stations
          fall on your head.
Desire machine
          moves to collage
              stiff spine

to buckled knees
broken heart to stellar debris
mothers pulling titties
from the mouths of babes tearing up books
endless reactions to endless infractions
move on
move on

Memoria Voraciae Simplex

Her clitoris
        the size of a Romanian pepper
     the feel of a leaf floating in silkworm drool
drops from the past:
            food or money honey?
Maria was from Somalia
          she worked on it a lot
   refined arabesque
pausing only
        to educate her taste buds:
  a dwarf politico
    on a wave of kif
      surfed in with nymph & satyr & boy & girl
      for each day of the week
      & one or two young poets.
In exchange
     she let him watch
    the tightening web
  his mosquito feet humming in the glue
   censor casting for a crew
    she would peel & train & ready
     to drown him.
To me she said:
      "I have only one enemy:
     MY THOUGHTS OF YOU"
I was young & scared: "Me?"
     "No," she said "Not you. My thoughts of you
your thoughts of me anybody's thoughts of her him & it!
Two thirds of my life
    I've been jailed..."
she opened two black arms & the wave grew
   "...by thoughts of you
    when actual contact
     is shorter than this song"
She touched it & it went bzzzzz hard & long
and the foreign army started to leave my brain
   I was a free man
          victim of electrocution
  as I spun down the road
         all sparks & zigzags.

The only woman
          I'm interested in
          is my mind
I later wrote her

On an Industrial Ruin

by underwood 378

A hundred beached
               Magellans of sex
                              blooming among
          layers of tires
crane their necks to look
                    at the first snowflake
          on vacant GOODYEAR
          "It is easier"
                    the snow says
          "to cover the sins of Baltimore
          than those of Newark New Jersey"
                    obliged to rage on
          until only one head
                              taller than the rest
          a black point
                    is left
          but not for long
                    to speak
          of something
                    it is yet to grasp
          but has already passed

Slot-O-Topia

Heavy coins roll down hallways
    we chase them
  & we catch them
  but can't lift them
    let alone spend them
but spend them we do
    beforehand
          in advance
    leaving
an arm
    an eye
        with the man
who has just
        given birth to a novel
he hasn't yet seen
          & does not intend to read.
It's there
    behind him
          bursting
with imaginary uses.
          It is unreadable.
  It is full
    of eyes & hands.
When the age of genius occurs
  & the future pays dividend
    & all those men who jumped
    from windows
        on Wall Street
rise from the sidewalk holding a new paradox
    but no
        structural mask
  for the bloody mess
they present
        to the startled pedestrians
when the lowly bureaucrat
    sheds his tweed & her pleats
& cries for worms
        in many languages
    or leaves
  & everyone undresses

          (a man-bird's worms are buttons
               on a rabbit-girl's wings)
     when the dead
                    & the near dead
          & those who are about to die
               eat of the light
     & stream naked from the hills
               into mailboxes
          (they fill them with feathers & fur)
               & give off much speech
                    to fill many ears
               which thank them
               "Thank you"
                         day & night
     with increasing gusto
          when all the modest spelunkers
               & the hunters
          & the money collectors
                    return from their caves
               stand up from their feasts
                    rise through the roofs of their banks
     & come to us
                         in the timely air bubble
                    (oxygenated pathos)
          to cure
                    our headache of sense
          when everyone stirs
                         & the windows open
               & the light falls on the bums
     & everyone who was crooked
               straightens out
          & a panther leaps out of each sweater
               to land
          claws out
                    on the phantom
          in every head

     a music will be heard
          of flesh pressed up & out
          by the return
                         of lost attention
     & the sport of light

(in progress)
plays on the torn membranes
making them cry:
"all we need now
is a pistol
a hat
& some shoes!"

In Praise of the New Russian Writers

to Vladimir Maximov on Farewell from Nowhere
& Alexander Zinoviev on The Yawning Heights

A Russian leaning with all his might
on what he doesn't know

a drunk against a poster on the wall
of a basilika in Nijni Novgorod

a silent nature full of poetic ideas
to whom words are tragic quantities

each one conscious of its literalism
coming out in the night to enlist
in an exquisite morality

perhaps a bowl of warm soup

answering as words are apt to
with their own sounds
when hoping to be fed:
we are here to testify against language

It is against this singular Russian
leaning with all his might
on our minds

we fill by satellite
with continuous hum the hollow night

Every Tie

Nobody's interested
(and how!)
in works-of-art-for-cash or:
nobody's afraid
(and how!)
of perception.
Nobody around here
gets to relax.
Nobody's the status quo, nobody's perfect, nobody is
not in sight, all we got here is production and
consumption production and consumption,
nobody don't see nothing not
if nobody is willing to be absurd
but will refuse to make immediate sense.
That's nobody's business.
Nobody's business is nothing.
To the question you ask:
"Does God exist or not"
nobody's going to reply:
"We answer in the affirmative.
Yes, God does not exist"
in the words of a bureaucrat
in midst of a news release
a *fait divers*
an epigram
an ad
an obituary
a curse
an epitaph
a mere fragment
of a bureaucrat
in need of a diploma
a court transcript
and a deposition.
Nobody here at *this* hour, pal.
Nobody opens the court for a deaf old bag.
The lost, the last and the list
(1920–1940 USA)
follow nobody around
for longer than that.

Nobody's in danger of becoming too hip.
When that happens
we contract paranoia of the normal
an intense horror of the Burger King
a couple of local nobodies
are discussing in terms of heaven,
a phobia of fried chicken
and we quit eating.
Nobody minds.

Horse Power

The world gets worse
life gets harder
pleasure is subject to quality control
no one in his right mind would refuse to shop
if offered the run of the mall

You don't know how to shop
You don't know how to drive
All you know is jive
Jive that keeps you alive
Dodging the folks sliding by
On greased tracks

Everyone I know does harm
The rich make little messes here & there
Then draw back
The poor wait & then kill somebody

It's so hard to stay awake
while screwing the earth & its fauna
in the name of the father the mother
& the horrible ghost
father drives mother drives
the son slides the daughter writhes
the ghost is up $1 & low
putt putt here comes the tree

Old world guilt machine
runs like a charm inside new world guilt '80
off we go to the land of suits Suitland

Here is Suitland
there are only babies & suits
babes in the arms of suits & armed suits
so let's talk business

Somewhere there is a race horse
made out of money
who must do his best
to lose the race

a total tax loss
who will eat a mountain of hay

I offer my literary acumen in lieu of this beast
guaranteed to lose up to any amount
in cash or in food
on the road or off
in my mouth & in those of my loved ones
& we will fuck the G-man but good too
I offer an abysmal and capable hunger
                          in place of doomed meat
I throw open the doors of my heart
                          to your tax dodges

Cool it mahn
or they'll never see the exquisite consommé
I hold open the doors of my better sense to
Your erect legal machine
until everyone's firm in the saddle

That's better

Off we go off we go
to this place I know

Baton Rouge & New Orleans

1986–1995

Dear Masoch

Dear Masoch doodling with his contracts
pens *Venus in Furs* on the margin of the document
he is preparing where it says
how many lashes he must receive, and where,
when the door opens & in the gaping doorway
a head framed by Viennese blue says:

"I am a Girl in Search of an Interpretation
filled with creamy snow like a vanilla éclair
I am waiting in the window of the dusty
European Poetry Shop for a soldier
to bring the following question before us:

'What do you do if you're a masochist but have been placed
in a position of power?' "

The girl who is the skinny international type
as yet unknown for another century
but whose prototype is already visible
in certain forward-looking writers like Madame de Staël
who is taking the species from courtesanship
to traveler's checks
hides behind dark glasses and travels with only a toothbrush
and a diaphragm in her straw bag,
objects unknown as well although their prototypes
in the form of rough twigs smeared with dental powder
and sea sponges soaked in torn anemones
have been in Masoch's house before.

She has power over boys and is equally at home with money.
He says:

"You must use your power to draw contracts specifying the
    amount
of prose I mean pain you want inflicted on yourself."

She is leaning on a cardboard structure waiting
for him to take her photograph and to sever the strings
by which the large balloon tied to the structure
is lightly attached and when sufficiently airborne

to take hold of her feet and kiss them.
The light of her soles flickers briefly above him
like the life of dreams flickers above all tales
& glows after they are told, for a second.
Her entire world is covered with graffiti. They say
Read Me. Interpret Me. He will. He does. He lifts the glass
paperweight holding down the poem and out the window
it flutters. Her damp pulse is in evolutionary
overdrive.
"They imagine they think" she says.
"I can get around reason as easily as Nietzsche
gets around his house to meet his fate. Or face,
as my mother says. 'You must have face!' 'With
face all things are possible!' If action is
the unreasoned interpretation of my position
whose oddity is beginning to bother me, then we are all
in the interpretation business. The reasoned
readings should, according to the interests
of the reader, be either weighed down or inevi-
table, so either let go of my foot or cut the strings."

It is a moment filled for Masoch with the rapture
of understanding nothing. Therefore he leans on the
poetic misappropriation of his youth by certain
aborted flights of reactionary romanticism
and pours out of himself:

"Oh, but I want to be thin and filled
with your doomed elegance like *filet de* swan, like
old verse in the corrupted daycore ... fancy
the daycore when I am through with you!"

The barely heard music of the threat is not lost
on the aspiring masochist. She too
is leaning on an obsolete tradition
instead of going to law school:

"A man furnishes his heart with explanation.
There, the chair. That's where the mirror goes."

"In a cheap hotel."

206

"So cheap I dread to think of the knives glinting
from the unbuckled belts of torn pants—men lurking
in the dim one-watt light bulb halls soggy
with blood their carpets still fresh from recent
beatings and forced strippings
the doors impossible to latch the windows painted shut
with an intoxicating lead-based paint
the bed sheets—what is left of them!—displaying
maps of *terræ incognitæ* in sperm and constellations
in blood drawn by either lice or the monthlies of
street women or forcibly taken virgins
and the constant hum! the screaming of busted
water pipes the moans of the dying junkie next door
the impossible visions of the nymphomaniac drinking in
three burly men at once, a fight on the street.
And then I see the terror on your face as you lie
under me being ridden like a nasty nag to your doom:
'What is the matter, scum?' I ask and follow
your terror-crazed eyes to the ceiling where they rest
on a monstrous *fleur-du-mal* painted on the ceiling
with human blood and brains. It appears
that someone lying on this very bed
put a gun under their chin or in their mouth
and decorated the ceiling thus. 'Oh!' and I can
feel it, the elusive gift of total surrender
as two prongs like a snail's horns shoot out of my
clitoris and antennalike begin to pick up the beat
from the far-off galaxy where I really live."

"And then just as my terror is transformed as well
into the pleasure of having fulfilled my contract..."

Masoch waves the contract in the air.

"...you get up pull up your little flowered undies
and leave, slamming the door behind you so that
a few chips of ceiling blood flake over me like snow
and I must stay there, like that, egglike
for at least fifty years until psychoanalysis
becomes a respectable profession and a psycho-
analyst a person one can call from a hotel
in the middle of the night, even in Marseilles."

"In all this," she says separately, to someone apart,
"Reason looms separate and voluntary like a fruit
in a rabbinical garden, or braces on the teeth
of Mormon belles. We are none too sure if the
Mongolians we imitate know how to read, and I don't
like yogurt. And I assume that reading,"

she turns the page

"is all there is, even if I'm awake. Especially
then. Can fresh water make it seem like next day?
I know who's listening and I came too soon.
The holes in spaces are purring like a cat, calling
attention to their idealism or their exactness.
They don't breathe too hard, or too slow, they are
not in a hurry, there is a universe next door,
a reversible fragment. Refreshed, after she slept,
Reason awoke to find Goya's monsters perfectly
appropriate, artistically drawn, and all that,
and in her mental baggage. Get those things out
of here! she cries. I will not rest until I make
an aphorism as good as those they have assigned
to me, and on she goes, I mean on I go, insisting
on the right to a nearly empty straw bag over
my shoulder, and a passport. I tell you, the original
mistake of philosophers is to keep silent
on music and on cars."

Misguided Masoch holds the trembling rifle he's been
holding for an hour, hoping to shoot Karl Marx. From
the dusty hideout in the fork of a twisted olive above
a farmer's pigsty, he calls to the thin shadow slowly
going from him like an effete oxcart:
"Untranslatable you! Banal futurism! Our paper servers
are combing the future for you! You are hardly
capable of understanding anything except your little
beastie-in-residence! You have been infected by the
legalization of pain and are no more than a bored fire
burning itself out in the bush alone, without a city,
firemen, great engines, excitement, and the press. The
overstimulated mind elite of which I was once part
is no more. We have taken to the twisted branches

of the olives with rifles. There is action in us! Oh
yeah! There is a kind of sleep in us from which
you will be born. I love you."

There is a brief report. A dove with a bullet in her
beak flies away. The two WWs in the form of two fat crows
stand on the branch above Masoch and chatter in frigid
vulgate. A caterpillar which is actually a grenade pin
pulls himself slowly out, and the explosion is loud
enough to eliminate the peasantry and rearrange the
geodemographics of the world. Of course, none of this
bothers Masoch. His name is immortal, and the contracts
he has drawn standard. The striped fields cross
the sentence in the hand-held word-mixer searching
like floodgates for the skinny psychopath from another
century who stands in her kitchen under a meteorite
shower mixing herself a Margarita. The urgency holds
her breath as she passes from the gates of metaphor
to the little Formica table where the sun shines
so lovely in the a.m. There is a chipped vase with
field flowers in it, some wilting, and a handful
of scallions rising next to it like the African
proletariat which never panned out. De-adjectified
she leans limply on the sill of her youth. She could
zip up her parka & mount the demented tractor still
and consider the transmission and love, which is
a motor function, but it is too late. The revolution
has subdivided her into dumber & dumber characters
like a trompe-l'oeil landscape composed of zillions
of theories, which she could think of as either
grist for the mill, or angels. In either case she
is a boss and an employer. Her passport has been
canceled, she can drink her drink overtly for the use
of money, or covertly for the repopulation
of the planet with tiny insectlike machine people
forcibly pulled out of the planetary psyche
which, empty, reels like a great revolver chamber
filled with the souls' ungraspable trajectories,
or she could *in extremis* call for her flesh
and for the bitter conclusion of her contract
with Masoch, which is death.

"None of that," she calls from the doorway
under the blossoming arbor where she has set
up an alternative to the hotel rooms of Marseilles.
"No dread sobriety should attend the gestures
of those present, no one should signal intently
to something out of sight, there will be no taxi
obscured by a tree with the motor running. No
furrowed brows ploughed under by thought, no
pajamas. No obvious seeds sprouting discreet
flowers, no discreet flowers at all. Only grotesque
flowers like one-eyed Susans, the floral Cyclopes. No
gents with violets, only gentians with mimosas. Only
uncertain professions, no new branches of mental
hygiene. No sulphur baths, no inception of chills, no
thermometers. No chilly languages, no translations
from chilly texts. No translators catching colds
from opening windows between languages, no crossroads,
only real stammerings, true hollows where the tongues
stand in their cases heavy with the awkward honey
of the first spoken, the as-yet-unsaid, the moist
dimensions, childhoods with animals, childhoods
that are great battles not preventive thoughts,
there on streets that can't exist, igniting
themselves with food mass-produced from all the nos
& no-nos a woman & her dummy can attract in a long
& unruly life, a river of charm, really."

Her voice runs from her like a monk pursued
by a buggering papyrus. Why are we not
in this book? cry her lovers. Because, she says,
without this time opening her chapped quotation
marks, those I love quietly do not textify
as readily as those who cause disturbances,
men like Masoch here, and other literary figures
whose photos I collect. All these guys do is
talk poems with big P as if the A-bomb wasn't
capital enough. Guided by styles, imagined
buildings, things impossible to draw, idiot
fantasies, wallowing in the rejecta of their
childhoods, they have originally happened
to someone else. To me they are semaphorisms,
crustaceans renegotiating the order of isms,

210

who have died for something in the future, some-
thing Sundaylike but juicy, the skin of something
basic and direct, why beat around the bush: me.
What good is the good horseman after he lost
his head? Plenty, say I, both the crazed horse
and the head that goes on thinking, rolling
crazed eyes at the border guard who wants to see
inside. They all want to see inside, it becomes
necessary to see inside every minute, then every
second it becomes necessary to see what's new,
or if the old is quaint yet, or if the dream
of lit has added anything since the oral rap
of certain marsupials. The fear is always
that we might go away before we figured out
why we came in the first place. That we might
run out of text in the flower of our youth,
not like Keats running out of youth in the flower
of his text. That we would crouch behind an unrehearsed
bit of prose, ready to pounce on the slightest
poem biking by, only to find that sentences
stretch into years, that years flow into pages,
that the world gets erased as quickly as we type,
that no one types, that a large gaze holds us
transfixed in its unblinking, flat look. You
really want me to put you in this book?

Having taken full advantage of her escape
from quotes, she stretches under the waterfall
of Masoch's steady penmanship under a backdrop
of Toledo swords and hears the pirouetting
of her shadow in his sleep, a sound like that
of a young Arab crouching behind a garage.

What legal needs I have, spoke Masoch from his branch,
which, used with the one below, served him
for the quotation marks he too had just escaped,
have been vastly rankled by the future
which responds only to forced entry and is
always the enterer, not the entree. Therefore
I'll charge myself a fee for every error of fact
and give myself a whipping for every odd fancy.
The State is a terminal cancer, it sucks

the lollipops of our souls, it sits on our skulls.
She does not exist.

Oh, but I do.

Music

There were no bums in my pores.
New York had opened my pores & bedenimed & bendovered
   walked in my fantasies
      shoving bums.
The stores were open and the hours late.
Expectations were being fed
      not sent to work
      like in far-away San Francisco.
I could speed up & slow down
   grimace & guffaw
      move my hands
         & look up to the lit windows
filled with admiration for the natives
   though not wanting to be asked in
since my living room at the moment was the biggest.
I was digging the streets & the streets dug me.
Every lunatic sped toward its co-lunatic.
Bellevue was lit up like another apartment building
   & in fact a party of sorts was going on
      with the inmates happy to be warm
         even as they were being hurt.
Ambulances piled in front & people went in & a few
      came out
   & the enormous hallways could have fit
      a Communist city's living rooms
         which they did
because on several floors the inmates slept there
but these hallways were dirty green & bright yellow
   & the neon was dirty
      & the unhappy floors
were track-marked by wheelchairs & police boots
      & mad jigs
         & flares & broken glass.
The floor to be sure was a picture of hell.
The prison ward was behind two tall gates &
      wire-mesh windows
         an easy jail break
& the cops were half cops & half social workers
      & in go the two poet workers
         with their two culture cops, i.e., books

& there are the prisoners
        half wanting to look at a woman
                & half desirous to look at free folk
    & half sick of each other
        & half sick
& half serious criminals
        wanting to improve their lot in life
& half mad criminals
        who had it in for the other half.
One came with a bed and a trapeze for his bandaged arm
        & half a body in a cast
    & another walked in wheeling a tall steel cane
on a flying saucer from which flew an IV bag connected
        to his arm
        & as he walked
        he recited bathroom walls
but was interrupted in midrhyme
            by an atmosphere of human color
            occasioned mostly by a reader of best-sellers
            who wanted to write them
because he had lived dramatically & was interested
    in technique & his interest
    led to metaphysical questions
        which gave the poets a license to interrupt.
Another was grim & tall & black
        & in his head he carried
the entire philosophy of an obscure mystical sect
            in severe couplets:
"In the middle of the pyramid there is an eye.
The dollar bill has a lookout in the fourth sky.
The steps to the Capitol are seventy-three.
That is the number to cross the zebra & the flea."
    I am probably being unjust
        to a grim mystical doctrine
            which the man whispered
                before being led out
                    by Big Sister
                        in midrhyme.
It was an evening to forget & one to remember.
It was 9:45 & the night was young.
At 10:25 I had collected myself sufficiently to return
    to the world hopeful

                & why not
when so many were rhyming the world in their heads
        even on their back & in bandages
& while you can't call this feeling love
        there being no room for close-up oppression
there was a hope that half was not lost.
Parts of the Sunday newspapers still covered the city.
The stores were open & a thousand ways to get high too.
Denizens of the night revealed fragments of wild costumes.
In the bookstores an intellectual orgy raged.
The smell of pastry & coffee was being attacked by ginger
        & Mongolian pepper
                from inside red restaurants.
It was possible to consume everything or nothing.
Either way the balance was righted
        the consumers as passionate as the ascetics.
The Lower East Side of New York
        moved eternally by a rhythm
"beating outside ordinary time"
                no shit
                        the graces of cheapness.
Cheap were the pirogis
        at the Kiev.
Cheap pirogis at the Kiev
        6 boiled with sour cream $1.95
a whole subclass converted to Ukrainian food
        & this without pamphlets
                or monks
each pirogi a pamphlet-monk
        doing its preaching in the mouth:
"if the Ukraine is ever to be free
                you must eat all your pirogi"
though there are people who do not like them
because they have first seen them fried
which is not always the best way to make somebody's acquaintance
not a pamphlet-monk's certainly
        & halfway through my second pirogi
                the radio said John Lennon was shot.
John Lennon was shot by an assassin.
Minutes later the radio said he was critically wounded.
And later yet that he was dead.
        The waiter held his plates in abeyance

                                                        215

& his face became very sad
& a tear fell on a pirogi
& I was still hopeful but shocked.
A man named Chapman meaning chap man man man anyman
"I am no man"
a failed double with a gun
a fallen half
had been shooting at a symbol & killed Lennon instead.
And now his music came from the sidewalks
& everyone understood
& became much sadder
& their tears fell
on solid gold pirogis rolling into image-making machines.
The symbolists had killed John Lennon
& I thought
look at it as a vacancy
a power vacuum
a king is dead
it will make everyone think
for a few seconds before commerce sets in
& that's no way to think
but it was thinking me.
Chapman was now in Bellevue where I had been
11:15 p.m. Monday, December 8
an hour earlier
with the other halved halves
& the hairs on my arms stood over the pirogis
when I remembered that it was here
in the Kiev
ten years ago
that I'd heard of Bobby Kennedy's death
which at the time struck me like the free winds of doom
with the apocalyptic illumination
of anarchist Jew
I owe to myself.
Ah cheap pirogis in love with yourselves!
I was in love but with no one in particular.

Dec. 22, 1980

When Lightning Struck, I

After The Pit, *by Frank Norris*

Genius
totality under partial control
a corner of the Market
part-time demiurgy

Then the waves come
and bury him in wheat

he couldn't rise to the job
when the earth took him seriously

Minutes later only a finger still shows
pointing to the clock
then it too goes under
a wave that feeds half of Europe
and drives a wedge between the American farmer
and his radio

He should have followed rhythms
not newspapers
though briefly they coincided
to do & undo him

Toward him comes the female of the species
and together they billow to California

to fight for a sincere blue reflection

When Lightning Struck, II

Petit Eros and J. P. Morgan

A little frigidity allows the mind in
A crack in the door
With mind comes a new kind of money
Soma spermica the unspendable
Funny money between each other's legs
Buttery beast music issuing from the earth
All the heroes get knocked up by their heroes
An imperative stands on the end of the nineteenth century
Like Angels on the tips of all those erections
Everything is urgent and cruel and industrial
Sweat wheels turn about the shoulders of modern girls
Lightning is a basic sentence the night is a book
Not yet remaindered the avant garde steps forward
A clamor for the moon overtakes the desire for saints
Movie stars purchase all the existing halos
Haley Muller Herschel Menelaus Nectaris Somniorum Tranquillitas
And sex is Muzak in Selena's mart J. P. owns
Homo sapiens turns into *Homo interruptus* WWI
Machines outdo themselves break down and weep
The hardwon hardons enter the Catholic lotteries
Genitalia swim & splash in the light of their own fantasia
The light comes on in the great white suburbs
To calypso beat of nymphomaniac drinking chemicals
The guy in op-art pajamas Mr. Morgan
Stands on the military lawn under a December moon
Of the next century   Behind him the door is cracked
In front of him two Frenchmen keep digging into the asterisks
Which are actually millions of people dressed by record companies
And pull out clouds of untranslatable bullion
Someone help me it's freezing out here he says.
He pukes out his gold libido egg.
Beginning in his tiniest earliest first person singular
A music advances into his hearing until he can't believe his ears
The acoustics of royal capital grow
Loading him with multicolored firecrackers
He swells to range over the Indian and Pacific Oceans
Impossible to pursue except by large generosity
Is lost for a few minutes in the equatorial belt

Which henceforth is destined to replace his pajama string
A rainbow for scarf   Infinity before and after
And is so vast finally he leaves the sentence
Bequeathing the earth to the smokestacks of his factories

Cohere Britannia

parallel coherent worlds   tectonic plates
jam and push up
that's no mountain that's the wedge of a perfectly coherent
world pushing up through this one like china through down-
town san francisco in the form of the transamerica pyramid
this sudden person under the window not there when i last
turned an intentional gaze into coherent scan is the advance
solo flag of a self-contained nation we know nothing of

suddenness is the signal of coherence incognito
subsumed by the typing hand which when withdrawn retires to
a place full of hands manuela tends
ditto the head
in the headarium subdivision is the full-time activity
time being in charge of its own linear coherence in charge as
well of what it contains conceiving it
never a dull moment

coherence in its own bag is being home
coherence in a double bag at the supermarket is being in prison
you boys better cohere here by the window
a coherent view of the yard leads to a better and more coherent
vision of things to come in a fine coherent world
cells cohere
coheres *coeli mundum*

lemme give you the coherent version of our position several
years ago me and a country i've never been in meshed whereby
i cohered into a society of former strangers and was reduced
to coherency not to speak tears having to constantly enforce my
and their coherency with clichés i got so much shit together it
uncoheres my anus to reflect the universe was one all this time
a one i held on to dug and grooved with all the coherence at my
side a sort of gilded lance and me saint coherence all set to
leap on two three four five and so on whenever things got nasty
in fact they were nasty one out of two fact being coherent by
virtue of corroboration
fact as coherence model
they had seventeen witnesses escapees from the local nut house
and one official in charge of capturing them who saw nothing

220

nota bene in the presence of any coherence please check to see
who is in charge then draw a map of the facts as you see them
facts tend to unsheet

all things become incoherent when incapable of defending them-
selves with maps i.e. unsheeted facts
coherence equals attention span
absorbed by a fly birds become incoherent to the ornithologist
the assumed coherence of the religious-minded young larry z.
makes everything everything and since he has no attention span
we wish him good luck in the hands of his faith
because he will have none at my hands which are now typing him
out larry who
all the coherence aphorism lent the world was lost when the
aphorist became a sonneteer
when god has logorrhea someone has to invent the haiku
a violet
blooms in his skull
the first flower of Spring

Petite Madeleine

We never discuss tenancy
We are a most peculiar couple
Our street isn't on the map

I remember kissing you
Form is punishment
The being compelled to it

Pays in full for the sizzling
Neuron grid clamped tight
On the cracked map

If you do what you think
You have to you can modernize
Yourself all on your own

Cooked in the end by micro-
Waves sweet fleeing monk
Buggered by papyrus

With first act of play on it
Performed by ancient photog-
Raphers in the loud mud

Of Egypt Mesopotamia Babylon
Dacia Illyria Thrace Baton Rouge
Mass-produced blowjob's

First Henry Ford a cosmopolitan
Criminal in Communist journalism
Walking to and fro in the glass

Aquarium of agents in the know
This street can't exist
So let's do it again

Doubling the windows and the bricks
Turning the vibrant hermeneut
Loose on the twelve-story building

Each story a bit peculiar
Self-told but totally dependent
On its mad teller's psycho-

Analysis like an I-told-you-so
Told in a thousand languages
A million inflections

Still what was it I told you
In the first place second third
I kissed you you had your orders

Volcanic Dirge & Co.

For E. B.

My life is all made into lit
Like some kind of raw material for export.
Until now "I" had controlling interest
Having nationalized the self for which
The only demand came from the forging of a taste.
Others could mine what they could use for spice.
And now you come along and corner the depressed
Market like Bunker Hunt.
You're welcome.
Loquacious before history
But speechless before talent.

That's understanding so I understand.

En Passant

Having avantbiographed the world
To make another come right out of it
I have certain scribbler's rights
On the next one—endlessly impregnate
The self about to be designed.

I praise the lava holes

whence issued my first passport.

The Inner Source

All good things
    eggs & hashish
come from Molotov's eye
    & return to Stalin's.
What I'd like to see
        he said
is a poem without Stalin.
    Me too.
There are certain kinds of typewriters
made for Ted Berrigan staccato poems—
    especially elucidating the question
of audience as singular.
                The same machine
addressing itself abstractly to a theme
    or a plural audience (also theme)
        would be more of a machine,
i.e., would be more æsthetic.
    Addressed
        to you
            it wobbles
betwixt the listening to itself & the void.
Likewise the telephone, said F. O'H., and true.
One gets his effects, said Lenin,
    from speaking to all as if all were one,
        thereby birthing the Hell's Angels.
But Stalin said
    entering the poem through the back
        that one must speak to No One
        as if all were included.
It never occurred to Homer to include No one
    though he invoked his guises.
And F. O'H. took to eliminating No One from the address
    by putting a name in the blank,
        an intelligent listening.
A great deal of whistling wind between a civilized
    address in a city with streets
& a steppe with hosemen picking teeth with lances.
Conquests instead of dentists
    oneness instead of arthritis.
Detritus humanists stash egg in the aortas.

A word sucked from the air and lightning
           spewed smoking out into the mouths
              of a million baby birds
                     versus
     the word ESPRESSO in neon and the rain
beckoning anonymously warm in Paris, France.
The verbiage of frozen butts upon the saddle of loud death
           sugar crystallized above the hush
              of cottony May evening *au coin*
                 du table.
History of what rounds (how many)
           and what babble
                 before specific address
and hey, hey, that was me talking
              to you walking
     away.
           Go on
                 while you still can
before they notice.
                     It is in this way
that the listener departed
                     a long time ago
           from an address in the city
changing his number leaving no telltale traces
              or tales.
The one Mongolian who tried was turned
           into thin slices and worn under the saddle
                 till pastramied.
The N.Y. Deli on Second proudly serves him now on rye.
Consequently only good Mongolians tell long tales.
           The epic-homosexual tradition
              survives intact
              in the unaddressed
              without address
              but tightly
                 packed.
The anonymous alienated prosaic use the full-page bourgeois
indigested aspirined and hebdo dramadaire Cointreau's sex
sated deconstructed (self) lophe
              tell toted (melted)
                 on the spot
     where addressed

where the telephone
was.
Imagine Stalin phoning up his troops one by one.
Imagine Mayakovski phoning up his fans one by one.
Imagine Dylan Thomas remembering each girl he fucked.
Imagine Whitman remembering each blade of grass.
Imagine Stalin phoning Mayakovski.
Imagine Stalin phoning Frank.
You can't imagine that?
Frank phoning Stalin?
Of course.
Let's talk mustache.
Let's hash the hush.

November 6, 1984

For R. K. on Rereaganization

History's can
   can only be filled
by brash moves
  not memory's trash.
He whipped his thigh as he spoke
   straightened out his tie
checked the spokes of his auto.
 History can only be
 produced as a design.
 In history people are
 elements of design.
 The hero whips in to
 restore the order.
 The world's a mess.
On Tuesday at 1:15 more or less.
 The heads pop. This evening
at precisely eight o'clock
Reagan's wrinkles will envelop the nation.
Anarchy's about to break loose. The made-up
President steps in
   his dummy walks out.
 A simian, somatic metaphor, whipped
  sleep, Apollonian zero,
   full can.

School Daze

Topaz extra: that's *stoned*
  Missed it in all the talk of ropes
      & animals.
Stoned among ropes and animals, wrote Ovid,
  get me outta here.
Those ropes and animals turned out to be my country
  for a few hundred years. Liked esp.:
  the cow, goats and sheep,
      and the poets, the flute players.
In the halls the flute players hold pencils.
They draw breasts with them all over the papers.
          Teacher, Teacher, what did I get?
          An A Breast, my pet.
Oooga! There is a tit on my test!
A toast to your tit! And so,
          he continued,
a city that isn't sexy is like ropes lying there
  in the old Black Sea port
after all the longshoremen died of clap
& the dusty statue of Ovid applauds all by itself
some Roman joke floating in from the Turkish coast.
But look, what's that? A cargo ship filled with
intellectual Nubians holding books by Susan Sontag...
      It can't be true: that's a flotilla
with all of New York aboard, including but not
confined to criminals, psychpats (that's pats
      you get in psych class), lunch-counter lizards,
    bus-stop toothpick types, bag ladies, cops, and bugs.
They are coming here to get out of New York.
They are going to disembark in New Orleans
          and continue on foot to Baton Rouge
where they'll become Ovids (a brand
      of cigarettes).
So pass the horizontal days atop the tilted nights.
          Eight days later
Time's house goes Bye

Comrade Past & Mister Present

Can the misfortune of a dog owned by vegetarians
be felt by a woolen creature exuding class privilege?
Looking through windows to glimpse tits I saw this
instead. It wasn't in the manual. But
applying private cures to collective diseases
occupied every page, it was *The Book of
the Transparent Tombstone*. You could see
all the heroes inside, and downtown Chicago,
men like Mr. Wrigley and buildings like the Tribune
Tower, and what they felt being there like that,
men and buildings squashed inside the look
of a drunk poet chased by wind
like a Sunday supplement on Monday morn.
You could read their desires but not their thoughts,
because you can read those like cigarettes in Lebanon
or Madagascar, and they said,
The thing to be is dead. Complete
thought evacuation. The cold wind
said that. The buildings themselves said
other things, having to do with stubbornness,
heart, commerce, stability, the will
of large men who know the world well
enough to sell it, and when.
You cannot throw up a building in Chicago,
my friend Debra says, and what, say I,
do I look big enough to throw up buildings?
Maybe my steak, but not a whole edifice, no.
You cannot, she says, do that unless it says
something, and buildings in Chicago say
some pretty strange things these days. I look.
They do. They say,
Choke, choke, have another drag,
then take a piss, warm water from the womb,
before starting to fire those tiny letters again.
A deaf woman with sign-language cards lurches
past a horn of plenty filled with writhing pretzels.
The deaf don't get fed here.
Not here now, a waiter tells her, and Gertrude echoes
from the wall:
There is no now now.

230

In France the dead gods were replaced by waiters
from many parts of the world, many grand waiters, former
czars and dukes and interior ministers
whose manners struck terror into the diners' hearts
and caused a form of socialism whose central burning
question was How do we put the pleasure back in the food?
I call the woman back and say, Ten cards! I have ten
nephews who need to speak your language. They live
in France. They operate a great Deaf Restaurant
where one day the cook chopped a customer's arm off!
On the same spot, a hundred years before
they guillotined a count under the eyes of his pastry
chef! And right now, at this very moment, as I sign,
the half-guillotined bourgeois extends
the stump of his patriotic arm to the former Bulgarian ambassador
(one of the cousins I just mentioned,
also a former Communist and member of the police,
but now a maitre d' and cook, and, secretly, a poet)
who holds it in the air above the slowly turning
rotisserie of history and orates thus:

At the present I cannot address my sentiments to the public,
because they will laugh at them, so I say to myself,
Scribble, scribble in the night, poet.
You are the sole mumbling interpreter of
an older art lost to the anxiety of the milieu,
a man from history, a faucet and a book, in a position
to know and to tell that
culture heroes are not characters, only private heroes are.
And you know also what's inside buildings people don't
really live in, in a country without directories.
But telling the truth after so many years of partisanship
is something I, the ambassador, cannot face.
But a roast, ah, that is incipience *and* fountain!

A very poetic busboy, a cousin I don't remember, streams
out of the kitchen sink
and cuts into the wounded grand bourgeois
and former commissar who keeps a chopping block
covered with parsley jutting from his torso
to keep hisselves apart (his
lacerations supple signs of philosophy):

When the great urge to testify came
pushing in like white water from all the rooms
without central heating, and even the railroads,
Monsieur l'Ambassadeur wrapped himself in the blank gaze
of speechless childhood, and was carted off, the coward,
into the virgin pages of a hospital. His revolver
became soft and impotent, and the great hum
of truth that was in the world looking for means
of expression became the generalized din of consumption,
a Berlin wall of televisions, fridges, and stereos
blaring out tears, pent-up sighs, wordless senti-
mentality, and something like physical symptoms,
which the world appeared to be, to him, in him,
and to the watchers. All around him, the cardboard
body of a huge Stalin was growing out of all
proportion to the photographer focusing in on his
tiny head. The editors of night, those antlike
monks in charge of trimming night to reasonable size,
swarmed about the edges of the pulsing heart of cheap
newsprint and tore out long columns of lies where, shattered,
lay the good gossips with their smashed complaints.
Hate-filled stars, asterisks pulsing, literature
called for blood. A stud in hospital slippers,
he moved from switch to switch like a wobbly line
drawn by a drunk engineer around a body dumping ground,
turning off lights, turning on fans, setting off alarms,
tripping over the mad logs, his colleagues, calling
for certain features of heaven with swollen tongues,
until he found himself before an exalted light pouring
from a stained-glass window, a veritable orgy
of colored light lavished on his puny and emaciated
person, and behind him was a black wood altar containing
an embroidered towel in which something twitched, and
a big, great electric fish on a sculpted ceramic dish.
I'd like to be outside, he murmured, but there was
no more outside, only this great weight of religion,
this oppression of God, and he looked up. His eyes
rolled upwards out of him as effortlessly as if they were
two eggs of brown light lifted by a spring breeze,
and were lost in the darkness of the Gothic spire's needle
injecting the blue sky with sight. He poured
through his vision, or in his vision, which carried him

232

like a rickshaw, into the darkness of the tower,
and became a liquid. The liquid that was sight, and
presence, and which the Great Syringe used hoping
to get the skies to lift their great empty chambers,
where God used to live, and make way for another sky
where He might still reside. And all this with the poor,
bulging, tired, eyeballs of a hapless ambassador
from the provinces who one day, in fear of mortality,
nearly succumbed to the great buzzing bees of truth.
Write this down, it's me, the busboy said it.

Aye, but he tells the truth,
the maitre d' he sigh.

Under these circumstances
a little populism is in order,
and the Socialists are just the ones to give it to us,
a little relief for Chrissakes.
Enough of architecture, more planning please!
Indignant, the customer rose to put the bill
into the ballot box, murmuring loud enough for everybody:
Dormir c'est souffler un peu.

Dumb but true, like all things evacuated
by the very truth they claim.
Cryogenics or dogma. Laws or institutions.
Contagion. Pleasure. Violence. Commerce.
The equator. Extravagance. Alaska.
"Just as the glaciers increase," said
F. Nietzsche, our good friend, "when in
the equatorial regions the sun shines upon
the sea with greater force than hitherto,
so may a very strong and spreading spiritism
be a proof that somewhere or other
the force of feeling has grown most
extraordinarily." So I take a good look
around, and see that brother Nietzsche was
right, as usual. All around us threaded
through the full-time simulation of pleasure
in which the world is presently engaged,
run currents of spuming black arts, the pin-
points of death maps all over them, everything

overlaid with instructions and written in small
print, in filigree, and at certain angles,
and they are shuffled & reshuffled every second
by great paranoid Shakers with both their hands
firmly on the boards and on the flippers.
Come see Commander Monko at the Koinonia,
he's from another dimension, and with him
are a hundred transparent beings eating human
jam with their X-ray hands, and he stands half
in and half out of a large green egg shouting,
What is it? What? Quick! Lie! Stand up! Breathe!
I came here to see how the store is, who minds
the store, one, two, quick, give me your watch,
it's not gold, no good, breathe! One! Two! Quick!
In Seattle the gurus met a few years ago
to discuss the weather. Not good, they said.
Whereupon the volcanoes, and James Merrill, all
erupted, and Edgar Casey bought a piece of Virginia
where winds don't blow, and great shoots of pain & light,
a wire mesh of symbols, slipped like an underquilt
under many parts of speech, including nouns but
mostly adjectives. Which left only the verb people,
us, to shift for ourselves as best we could, dodging
the illusions of the insane mass, and their cabbages,
æsthetics, engineering, and embryos.

Engineers fix up the dried-up mug of the President
with beer. On another billboard
her thighs move slowly to engorge our willing selves.
A pall of sleep lies over us. Occasional violence
wakes up somebody to fun, fucking, fanfare, form,
the full five minutes of total squirming by which
the mess augments and rips things like cloth and materials,
silk and underpants and London Fogs. It's like
a turning upside down of Apollinaire's heart, to spill
all the love on us, *coeur renversé*, like fairy dust
or cocaine, forever, and with little golden lights in it,
light aphorisms for the abruptly airborne, and the slowly
rising. Dig it here, outside it's all but gone.
Funny how the butterfly Chuang-tzu, a reversible fragment,
insists on the prose of myth and will not,
under any circumstances, recover history for man.

234

Funny how he and other of angelic ilk get by
both the historical and the ideal, proceeding upwards
from this particular man here,
a horny bastard, lost the night entire,
having whiskey, mustard, cocaine, like I said, and great fountains
of words in Blarney's Bar, to the scattered applause
of two fat cops in drag revolving on their stools, over-
sized ballerinas at the Musée Grotesque. These are my
mustard brothers, he proclaims, and these my mustard
sisters, yielders of great big keys fitting the great big
doors of the decades, slammed shut upon the continually
retiring mustard seed of the soul, a firefly, in the dark
tower, with a book and a regret. The book, by Nerval,
flows like the neon above the tired square, nothing
but porn at this hour, and a limp chain or two over sweaty
leather. One can easily see Huncke here, and his Beat
friends, tourists, checking out the night in the interests
of literature, and Soviet critics bent on vodka. But mainly
he enjoys the particular eddy he creates, the swirling
thick mustard of fraternity, and the outside chance
that difference is yet in the world, enormous, if perilous,
and the clashing currents roaming the night may yet
proceed in the direction the twentieth-century *bohème* sketched
out for the collectors and the fools, a direction made
necessary by its being, alas, the only direction not leading
to the Camps and to the Army. *Le Paradis n'est pas
artificiel* but one must have an alternate hell, or go
with Mr. Lowry to the Farolito, or with Doubleday to
the remainder pit, not to mention Hitler & the rest.
There is no talking that does not lead to this, and to
little plays based on this, and the tap dancer jumped
on the table and made a great dance of this based on
the songs on the radio, eyes closed, feet beating the
Formica with the message that he was here, and he was
glad to be with us, and we were there too. It was a Morse
novel of feet calling and describing all of presence and
its necessity, a beat of forgetting and insistence
on the now, and a firm, albeit desperate, reiteration
of here as being here, I mean there then, here now.
The time has clearly passed for the partisans of now.
If they, we, want to make their, our, presence felt
we have to greatly beat our feet on the ground made

from the heads of our contemporaries filled with
oblivion gas or, worse, detailed visions of exactness,
maps of the very heads they describe *and* fill,
and then hope that the desperate beating in a prose
so beautiful as to wake the lit crit in every heart,
lying (alas!) disconnected from the gas-head at the feet
of some other entities with which we rarely if ever
converse, will reconnect head and heart thus causing
the layer immediately beneath (the great
ontological floor, O Mintho!) to, in its turn, begin
to beat its, their, feet on the heads of those below,
and so on, through all the many cavernlike interiors
of the baby cosmos, until exhausted, intoxicated,
and utterly ecstatic, it meets the Great Outdoors
and their symphonic No. Or Whatever. A real job,
if ever I get one.

The great discovery of my thirties is plurality.
Don't guffaw, Maurice, please listen now.
All my life, and that includes the half of it
which is distinctly literary, soon to surpass in sheer
numbers of years all other, I have thought,
along with babies, bishops, Copernicus, and Sartre,
that one's job in letters and in life
was to express a self attached to a head
which can then be detached, cut off, *tu sais.*
I tried to stumble my way out of the box of self
as best I could, given the orders I had, which
included complete directions to every museum
on the planet, but found myself creating monads,
perfectly selfish little globes of soap, not firm
like tits, nor smooth like spheres, horrid new
energy to propagate themselves concentrically
through life and lit and sometimes through the park.
Which is not, as I see it now, the point.
The point—put here your place names with Point—
is Plurality, Point Plurality, to be exact,
a landmark that's been here all along, on which
Mr. Jefferson grounded us and made us a building
at Monticello, in Virginia. Point Plurality, almost
exactly the way it is in Mr. Murdoch's papers,
and in these buildings from the days before

taxes, modesty, civic restraint and fake humility,
and the way all noble rhetoric would have it,
including my citizenship lecture and the loving
drunken bash afterwards, in other forms. In other
words, all other words, not just the tolerance
of difference, but the joyful welcoming of differences
into one's heart spread out like the pages
of a newspaper. The pursuit of the dialectic,
as Monsieur l'Ambassadeur would say, without which
one cannot live, although, alas, it is much harder
to practice in words than in the kitchen.

For you, I said.

He handed me back my arm.
Whereupon I grasped tightly my cliché and thin-lipped
went through the door into the street
where the small animals are barbecued.
I did enjoy the pale winter sun.
I made the most of the spring breeze that lifted minis.
I let my tongue wag into the summer heat and collected
a whole urn full of lovely sweat.
In the fall I fell with the leaves and was *désuet*.
Winter came to take me to bed.
Streets, cities, waiters, and parades—
these were the hair my various barbers chopped,
falling in great profusion into place, exactly
where they belonged or not. So using the conveyance
of the "I" to get us through the streets I came
to the exact meeting place of a thousand "I"s
clamoring for attention with an uninterrupted
belief in culture and the Pie.
I hovered there until I found you.

It was no ordinary party. Ted Berrigan was there.
Anselm too. And so were all the great orators of
our time and theirs, and a number of philosophers
in the corners, with that corned-beef look in their
deli eyes. And the music was L O U D! I mean,
we rocked! But for all that, you could hear
every word and our voices were nearly alien
to us because that unnaturally low or high pitch which

we acquired in order to talk above or below music
was nearly gone, and we spoke the way for thousands
of years people spoke, without the din
of perceptual cultural imperialism, but clearly
in the din of the market only, if we so chose.
I mean, when we wanted din we went to the market
and talked so the policeman wouldn't hear us.
The world is louder but the policemen listen better.
The old chickens squawking and the screaming gypsies
were as good as nature when we needed cover.
Like I say, we were both loud and clear
and happy knowing both schedules and eternity,
simultaneously upside down and horizontal
like bars on a music sheet in a big bed!
But there were some gents and gentians on the canopies
who looked as if they'd eaten the green apples of jealousy
and then OD'd on the wormy peaches of reason,
embarrassed recipients of large grants and prizes who
had removed themselves from human company.
One of these, a pathetic necrophiliac with spindly legs,
said that when the mind matures the sentences
come fully fleshed, in erect glory, and indeed
a full-fleshed sentence hung at half-mast from his sad
erection. It was *I paid for the gas so where am I?*
There are these bummers even in heaven, close even
to the mystery itself, not too close, of course, for
fear of being burned, but close enough. They sit or lounge
within sight of the mystery itself, scribbling on, not
seeing it. Once in a while they stop dead in their tracks
and wriggle as if the devil was in them. What happens is
that the mystery has a public-address system and it broad-
casts spontaneously and for fun, to blow their minds.
The mystery with in-built megaphone came thus to Lorca,
Mayakovski, Hikmet, and Ritsos, but not in translation.
Most times, however, the mystery whispers, depending
on attention for its erotic food, which it demands
without fail, to keep its flames fanned. "Our job," said
brother Blaga, "is not to uncover it but to increase
its mysteriousness." And so the mystery burns
giving off only enough light for the enormous job
of making oneself. Each time, every night, all
experience must be renewed. Others' successes or

failures are of no importance. The flames are not
bookish, and the sooner you give a child his or her wings
the sooner they'll get on with it, and that is how
from generation to generation the overprotected rich
get weaker and overprotective tribes lose their sense
of hearing and their anger, and they begin to cater
to the dead. The dead lie like a heavy book cover
on us, our tombstone. It is their business to take
our time, to oppress us as much as they can, until
we say everything for them and train others to be dead.
They blackmail us every minute, so fuck them!
Must we always, like mad Swiss bankers, synchronize
what happened then to what happens now?
I'll write the poetry I always wanted to, or none at all.
The conventions of my generation, life, teachers,
lovers, maps, cars, music, art, the things I've said,
fuck 'em all, ploys clearly of the anxious dead!
The content that fills the flowing shapes
of my heart's pure yearning is communal like the city.
A fraudulent but real place like any other.
The infinite and the political do not exclude each other.
The particulars of a face need not break the concentration
of desire. *Au contraire*, they could augment it. And
in psychoanalysis and other therapies, people pay
for what they are missing, and not in order to recover it,
only to be confirmed in their lack, to be reassured
of the normality of absence, of the utter popularity of
the abyss, the sanctioned nothingness, the triviality
of death. Oh, we were vacated by the gods, they cry,
so we had to put language in the hole! Or waiters!
Well, I prefer the mask to the well-thought nothingness,
as I have said before, and I only took this job because
no one is doing it. The job always, the only job,
is to be an ontological reminder, a real pain in the
ass, reminding everyone why we took up the pen
in the first place, to scratch ourselves on the wall
or under the aching arm, to kick open the lid, to set
the water free, the hair loose, the spirit flowing.
Make you hear again that metarooster crowing!

After I had my soup a fat lobbyist, selling satellite
contracts to Indian and African businessmen at the next

table, took football jackets out of his satchel
and presented them to the grateful foreign nationals
who interrupted their scheming on how to get their
countries' treasures to Switzerland, for a minute,
and said, The Raiders! Yeah! Yeah! We love the Raiders!
I interrupted my meditation and thought of Salvador
Dali, how it is possible to praise this world and
plunder it, without renouncing either others or the next.
I also gave a brief thought, because my curry was late,
to Kant's disciple Fichte, who said, "The Not-I is the
product of the I," a truly egocentric take needing
an instant Galileo. On the other hand, and here
I fiddled with my spoon, without the consciousness
illuminating the big It out there, how are we to see
it? By the neon of Chicago, natch! And then
the curry came, and it was hot, a red mountain atop
a purely golden bed of rice surrounded by little opal-green
islands of onion and mango chutney, and warm hissing
flat breads giving off air bubbles, and hope. The I
is neither product nor originator of the Not-I. That is
posing the problem falsely. The I is the enemy of
the Not-I, its colonizer, conqueror, and exploiter,
and here I dove into my food and was fierily gone.
The I is in the business of substance sucking, de-
sacralizing all the routes and getting fat.
The Unknown is my food, and that is that. I take
my rest at the Richmont Hotel and have my hair
groomed, and then I walk. There are
people who wish to show their solidarity with their
fellow creatures. Others want only to display
a spiritual difference. My company is with
the former but my sympathies with the latter. After
the light comes the odd turn, then the giant feather.
In the warm lobby I find the latest newspapers. I sigh
for Carmen at the cinema. Oh, close my word-weary mouth,
you arch, cross, vaulted, fleeing Gypsy slut!

A Brief (Remembered) *Histoire* of Rejection

THE TRICK

To make daylight. To put a mirror in front of the Thinker: to occasion Narcissus to meet the anus. To have them speak to each other (through the heap of junked structures in which they squat) in hermecholalic masomaneuvrable slang (*the hermetic/hermaphroditic echoing echo of what has been left out of language through the maneuvers/manipulations of the masosocial contract.*) To reach into the sleep of the race for the forgotten, the rejected. To send the self (shaped as a bomb) into the shit pits. All the archlogs & archeologues of rejection to report to me by four. Over & over until no one shows up (in the dissolved heavens authority comes up over & over, and over & over form the rejected heavens). Society is the product of rejection. It is the form of what it doesn't want. Its borders are carved up by the weight & pressure of what it has thrown up/squeezed/pushed/puked/killed. To dredge the outside back in. Dredgers to join diggers here by four o'clock. Dredgers to turn the glove inside out. Diggers to go down into the dream shit pits of the race.

REJECTIONIST COSMOLOGY

In the beginning, a spaceship flew by. The alien astronaut, disgusted by the monotonous diet, threw his half-eaten sandwich down on the black rock they were passing over. The sandwich fell on the rocky blind orb and proliferated. Humanoid germs came out of it carrying little meat suitcases with Swiss stickers on them. Eventually—after the passing of many pullulating centuries known melodramatically as history—the germs began to remember their origins and to have ecstatic visions of their home in the alien sandwich. Slowly, in a concerted but unconscious effort, they commenced returning to an original state of primal garbage. When they were all buried in the waste products of their dream of Eternal Return, they were seized by an inexplicable but perfectly stupid sadness.

TO REMEMBER

The politics of memory. The state of memory. The unremembered, the exiled, the banished. The citizens of the State of Memory: Images of Success. Tito shaking hands with the Yankee bandit. Stalin & Roosevelt carving floral meat lumps on the map,

241

their shoulders touching. Mother feeling good, a rose in her teeth. Father away for a week, the town squares abandoned to dream in. And outside? Outside memory? All the alien organs, the undulating terror, the ejected Rejections. Far in the Horizon (ten four, over) are the Great Rejections looming up like the stones on Easter Island. The ancestors. They are the Rejections involving more than 51 percent (controlling interest). They have been exiled so that the body (locus of shifting I's, beehive of I's waiting to swarm the flowers... ah, Rose, your body is Jesù!) may survive. Weighted down with Oblivion, pretty good stuff, eh? The Rejection of Rejection.

The Three Bodies of Oblivion

1. DISBELIEF

Common, diurnal, regular, average, axial, knife-shaped, shish-kebabed first body (weapon) in the three-word vocabulary (arsenal) of Rejection of Rejection. He calls you "pig," and you must disbelieve. See all the victims of malfunctioning disbelief? Half-human, half-pig, they wallow in the plugs in the Urbis & the Burbis. Good Functioning Disbelief, on the other hand (with the other hand) takes the "pig" out of quotation marks and makes it part of the little Rejectionist Zoo each citizen ought to operate. There, the pig joins other scornful beasts, named after the animals we have exterminated, whose forms of being we have rejected: hyenas, imperialist dogs, dodos, turkeys, slimeballs, worms, ostriches with heads in sand, donkeys, parrots, snakes. It is a National Holiday and all the children are visiting the Inner Zoos, holding onto their parents' hands, prior to being rejected for looking.

★Warning★: *Disbelief is nocturnally nonfunctional!* Literalism (dreams) takes its place. At night, you must push the pig through another door yet.

2. LITERALISM (DREAMS)

Goods news, folks. All those people considered lost over the years & under things have been found. They are in dreams. Turns out the dream's the greatest employer hereabouts. All the rejected— we just call 'em lost to go easy on you—have good jobs in dreams. There is only one job actually but everyone shares it:

242

dredging. Dredging up, that is, to an ever-transparent surface the bodies of those who have dreamt themselves below all contact with language. Those statues on Easter Island are towers of language, grown enormous with the articulations of power. The power they need to pull out the bodies they are always about to pull out. The bodies they pull out are also pulling them in, with all their strength. Rejected themselves millennia ago (lily mollusks rainbow machines) they are rejecting (with all their might) the entreaties of transparency. What they mistake for entreaties (seduction) is actually brute force. The ancestors, both above and below, are very tired. Thus they are slow & often do no more than tug gently at each other & wish for Total Oblivion (the Three Bodies Thereof) to cause one or the other to float up or down. They half-dream themselves of others, lost in their dreams. A progressive paralysis invades the dreamer, flowing in like a wheel of lights.

3. IMAGINATION/DEMIURGY/POESY/INTERCHANGEABILITY

The mythical/collective/legendary incarnation of Oblivion. Vertical to Disbelief & Dreams which lie flat on the Diurnal & Nocturnal, balanced uneasily on a wavy line drawn by the drunk Mr. Hegel as he stumbles Home. So drunk he does not see the lamppost, vertical to the sidewalk he had trod so cheerily the other way only this morning, looming in front of him with the matter *dolorosa* of his brains about to be handed back to him. In this lamppost, shedding an imitation of day inside the German version of night, the two planes are reconciled, chewed up in an unrecognizable pulp by electricity, to look good & digestible for eventual reconciliation with consciousness itself. The chewed-up pulp of day & night we continue to improve on is going to— upon impact with Herr Hegel—affirm the Totality. My poesy, said the poet, as he helped the unconscious philosopher to his feet, is made up of the chewed, indigestible, unswallowable material of Rejection. So when the poetry itself is rejected (by guardians of the word cage guarded themselves by invisible censors with Shakti cattle prods), I am sent flying backward on the diurnal-nocturnal planes to reverse the gravitational axis, annulling, momentarily, all the Original Rejections. Affirming, in other words, the being forced to such deviousness. For a moment—in the rejection of my chewed-up rejections—I am made whole. My first reaction, enthused the poet, to the rejections of my poetic creations has always been one of extreme exhilaration. In that moment I stand affirmed. What I have to say—the doctored ancestors, the pinned cell, the dream amoeba thrashing in the word net—has touched the limits of the world. I've come to the end of the world. To the end of what is known. *Au bout du monde.* Everything around the known world (the tiny, as in medieval geography blowfish world) is rejoicing at the arrival in the World (outside the Perception Curtain) of a New Poetic Monster, a Dæmon, a New Substance. Livid vivid putrefacta. My creation, ah. Livid Vivid Putrefacta Rejecta. The poet threw his arms around the moon—dropping Mr. Hegel—and found himself embracing a cliché. Word garbage men picked up the sheets of paper flying behind the pair's uneasy progress Home.

3/6/81, Amtrak

Bridges with empty niches waiting for rural madonnas.
Subjects of somebody's nostalgia. Not mine.
The backs of old Pennsylvania towns. Rusted boats.
Rococo iron grille. Car garbage. The beginning
of the century. The fantasies of children watching
from those windows. The new house backs are the saddest
of them all. A solar-paneled condo. Silos. Dutch
paintings. Cows. Tykes with waving kites. Old
church roof like ruffled nun's headdress. Black
flying saucers on the fields: the hats of Amish
farmers behind six-horse plows. There is a woman
in one of these houses with their backs to the train
who exposes herself to the 5:29 from Chicago but
the glare of the sun in the window blinds us and we
don't see her. She has her orgasm at 5:31 on the dot
just as the linkage on the last wagon flashes by.
She's been satisfied this way for twenty-one years. Her
husband doesn't mind. Old rusted disconnected rails
right by our side like Morse code. Displaced
consciousness like suddenly seeing your head next to
yourself. Hospitals high on the hills. Closer to God
I suppose. Françoise Nicole Depuis liked the train.
From it she saw a lonely stretch of road in lovely
pasture country. There there she thought I will open
the best French restaurant in America. Françoise
is the daughter of Master Chef Depuis whose cooking
rated so many stars the Michelin gave him his own
Crab Nebula. At ten she had been drilled in Brillat-
Savarin & at fifteen she easily outcooked her father.
The little clapboard shack Françoise acquired was
an easy fifty miles from the nearest town in the heart
of Amish country, people notorious for liking only
their own food. Françoise hung up a sign that said:
FRENCH RESTAURANT, Françoise N. Depuis, PROPRIETOR
and then she waited, waited, waited, waited, twisting
now her starched apron, now the lace of her slip that
showed and showed. A week later the J. C. Penney salesman
working that country entered. She made duck *orange*
from personally caught duck, steak *au poivre* with
pepper brought by her father from the Côte d'Ivoire,

two soups, one sad and one happy, i.e. one that made one
weep and one that made one silly, a bisque, and for dessert
a torte, seven éclairs, and two napoleons.
The man ate everything. He thanked her. That was
nearly three months ago. Françoise is waiting. Won't
you help out little Françoise? The backs of charred
factories. Oily ponds with lotus blossoms on them.
Mercury water. Tufted islands in the Susquehanna
River. The four towers of Three Mile Island. A farm
house right next to it. And another. Cows. Sheep.
The "Art on Reactors" program of the National Endowment
for the Arts has painters and sculptors in the area
painting & sculpting grotesque masks, Aztec, African,
Egyptian, Soviet, Granadan, Cuban, Jewish, & American
to be affixed to the outside of the warm cooling towers,
to make them the true objects of cult horror we know
them to be. Death gods. Serial billboards run along
the highway running along the tracks. God in
installments. AFTER LIFE WHAT? A mile farther: DEATH.
A mile more: AND THEN? In one more mile:
THE JUDGEMENT. I note that everyone who is not going
to Chicago stands now, and they are wearing thick
belts painted with the Stations of the Cross. Silos.
Rich pastures. Silence. The fat Yugoslav conductor
steps forward with a radio, and the fat setting sun
blares forth from it. Beauty, it blurts, hurts. Beauty
hurts because it's subject to instant nostalgia.

246

A *Petite Histoire* of Red Fascism

for M. Brownstein

All connections
are made by energy.
The inert masses
know nobody & not
themselves. Nobody &
Not Self are well worth
knowing but connecting
them takes energy
so they are known
only by their masks
of inert proletarian
matter—Bolshevik
statues. The people
with the most energy
employ themselves to
know the statues. The
statues are well-known
by the inert masses.
The people with just
a little less energy
are then employed
to interrogate the inert
proletariat. One energy
grade below, the police &
mental-health apparatus
employ themselves to
energize the inert mass
which is now for the
first time broken up
into individuals.
Breaking it up releases
energy—enough energy
to respond to questioning.
The police level then ex-
tracts a primitive narra-
tive from the recently
inert & this narrative
generates enough energy

& excitement to produce
a two-level discourse which
makes sense to the upper
energy level. New
energy is created & soon
the top echelons are
introduced to the dis-
courses of Nobody &
Not Self. Together,
the brass & the mass
envision the statues:
the energy of the mass
will henceforth be em-
ployed to make statues
of the brass.

Belligerence

In the irruptive mode
I wear no hat
& hate what I see
in the rearview mirror
except silver balls.
When I was all the rage
I was in disruptive mode
& wore the instructions
on my Reeboks to a frazzle
between the lines of what
everybody read and the high-
way stripes painted there.
Actually shoes in those days
had no names but I was futurist.
Mealtimes at Hojo's & Wendy's
the plastic tablecloths
had squares in them and squares
in them and the prices were cheap
obsessively and people
in those days laughed
until their faces
became tic-tac-toe boards
& few could tell death to shut up.
Life was no fucking (pre)text.
Menus with everything under one
dollar were not unknown.
Anyway, only the greatest
could write it down. I was
among them. Since then, volcanoes
were miniaturized,
everyone gets to be
a little sick. I know
everyone who works here,
they are not happy.
I wear a dunce cap.

Circle Jerk

Nel mezzo del camino I found myself
in the middle class
looking at two diverging options:
ideology and addiction.
My triumph is to practice both.
Revirginate or Perish!
Learn how to read to trees!
(You never know who might be listening
when the class enemy is in the class.)
Can he be that hombre
who walks into town
followed by a slow caravan
of Toyota vans laden
with empty mail sacks
ready to BUY EVERYTHING?
The shelves, the things on them,
the stores themselves,
the clerks' personal effects,
watches, homes, mothers?
And gives them
whatever they ask for?
When this hombre leaves
the town wobbles like a great
plucked chicken
and shivers from cheap wind.
This hombre then sits
in on a card game
west of the Pecos
and tells this joke
to the members of the Cabinet:
An old Jew asks the Soviet
border guards for a globe
to see where he should go.
After hours of careful study
he returns it & asks:
Do you have another globe?
In the end we remember not the joke
nor the out-of-place place where
he tells it to the people
but the fact that we all detest living

through the adroit manipulations
of the small-print clauses
of our social contract.
Therefore you in the front row
wouldn't you rather
Do It Your Way?
Don Juan, narcissist
whose job is to upset order
and the authority spent
establishing it,
releases energy
teased into being
by his hat.
Once a man loses his taste for himself
he becomes completely unsavory: meat
spoils from within.
Others seep in through the chinks
and chomp chomp their way through heart & gut.
Two careless lovers are worth one thousand bankers.
The world is froth over the surface
of an untouched hard core
that first looks real,
then nostalgic, then Betamax.
I stagger from BBQue to BBQue
& never see sobriety anymore.

Seeing out of the Sub

for Alice

How do you see out of a sub?
I feel like I'm inside a sub, you say.
I feel like I'm inside a sub too.
The iron blimp in the Cabildo,
the confederate sub, possibly
the first sub consisting only
of a large iron body with a propeller
and a blind mariner inside her
hoping to ram a ship from underneath.
The mariner's hopes were the end of him.
Maybe it's best not to see out of a sub.
Maybe it's better to have a party.
Jonah's had rooms for millions.
The metaphor, I mean.
Maybe what we're inside of is a metaphor.
For the middle class, for instance.
The middle class is most like a sub:
Squeezed from below and squashed from above.
Despised by poets just like a shark or a sub.
I think what we need is a pun:
Remember the Chinese sub on the only
sleazy street left in Baton Rouge?
How we sought it out and delighted in its urban
cheapness? Its meat-filled blandness with lettuce
and the window where nobody sat?
That was a good place to look out of
because nobody cared what you were looking at.
The Chinese were busy eating their own product
when they weren't making more.
Our product, interest, and an interesting world,
comes about with looking like that
out of the window of a cheap sub shop.
The raw material is looking and looking.
It's no good being blind in a sub.
It's good watching from the sub shop.
The metaphor must yield to the pun.

Virgin Mule

The conversations of the French
Quarter mules in their stables
after a full day of pulling
tourists and voters over cobble-
stones is not espresso witty
and in their dark no TVs feed
them news of the ends of mules
elsewhere in the Middle East
and West. In our stables the ends
of others are a fact of atmosphere.
The yoyos on the mystery island
next door are revving familiar tools
in backyards now gripped by failure
first of electricity then of
a meaner something that'll grow
into nothing we'll know in the A.M.
Once they were visitors like us
then they grew mulish in their
bubbles and pulled whatever
was put around their necks in-
cluding a banner that said, About
What Kills Us We Know Little.
On certain nights after a good
internal fight we hear the voice-
less others through the glass
fearfully sweet'n'soft like dough.
Oh let the monsters in. Help us
rise above our not seeing them,
may they let us into their eyes
as well. Banish the blindness
of these cobblestones, clop, clop.
But! Pffsst! Our notes are in-
complete. Loving you was
never on the agenda. Better
to sing as roughly as the stones.
On Memorial Day we had one
thousand hotdogs & counting.
Didn't visit a single graveyard.
We the Grant Wood folks scan
the sky for incoming missiles:

253

blips ourselves we understand
timing and touring in America.
The gilded dads in the portraits
sought the idealized continuity
now moving before us democratically
in showers of pixels and dots.
I'll go with the distracted mariner,
my lover, and we'll be in the world.
It will be late by then and dark.
We lyric virgin mules keep our
book of hours in a dream apart,
having stranded a billion turistas.
But we could not break the chummy hand.
Ready to brave the snow without a hat,
severe weather notwithstanding,
we merely nod and understand.

Telyric

Stand here, says the professional TV person.
She shields me from the sun with a silver shield.
The nuclear-trained soundman wires me to himself.
"Had top-secret clearance," he says,
"Shut four years inside a sewer pipe. Bad only
when the dope ran out."
"Top-hat clearance?" I ask.
"Our army's stoned and theirs is drunk."
A geezer stops: "He somebody famous?"
He spits in the fountain of the Immigration
& Naturalization Service said years ago
to have been an object of controversy
capable of shielding terrorists
in the goldfish rolls of its Dubuffet clusters.
The British cameraman who shoots me is proud
of his tee-shirt from which a Scandinavian
plastic surgeon named Tord Skoog
rises blankly from humble beginnings
to an obituary in the *Scandinavian
Journal of Plastic Surgery*, and from there
unto thousands of tee-shirts
from Patagonia to Maroc.
My telyric self bends in the sun-
solitude of its large puppethood.
A window of light is in the dugout roof
concealing the new national hero of Nicaragua,
pitcher Dennis Martinez.
I am connected with wires but not to sense.
The girl waves her white arm with the lamp:
I walk to her across the narrows
of my TV-less childhood.
Go on, put on the shield.
I throw the first pitch into the sun,
my tinfoil trembles like Skoog's fjord.

Leaves of Nerves

Nylon is a wonderful thing in a city with trees.
Inside the wilderness of self
is outside but outside
is still inside
for Mr. Smith from St. Louis
who phones
to say all night I was inside
his head. "I was hoping
to speak to your message machine."
These are the very rich hours
of the Middle-Aged Duc of Poesy.
Onward & beyond
to the times when one would like
to write through
the machinery,
namely the love current,
but how much one belongs in the world
depends on how brightly
one talks to the police.
The aggression of health is badly understood.

The Introduction

After the interminable play
the beautiful actress
landed on him, a balsa plane
of starlight and dust
& asked to be presented
to the famous director.
All cities are Paris.
He effects an introduction
in a language no one
even pretends to understand,
Kurdish-Magyar, and night falls
about the yurts & colibas
as star & cast go off to the clubs.
He goes on & on explaining
why he is rooted to the spot,
an olive in the desert
but his listeners also
have their hands stuck
in front of them like branches,
olives too.
They are in fact a grove
where the philosopher walked
one noon. They have since then
imagined themselves right into
our century, in Paris.
What was at first chasm
became mountain then Chaos-town.
Theatre will never be the same
though the Japanese arrive in droves
to kill themselves beneath their shade

Demands of Exile

for Dorin Tudoran

We are growing a bitter seed issue
of poets who can't go home again
in this here jar of a mag. Here are
squat men in fat suits papillon greasy
huddled in dark Chicago basements
perched on writing tables to leap
to Paris into Biedermeier inkstands.
Prettiness of course isn't the issue
when one has left behind all the pretty
things and is now at the mercy of scents,
happenstance, emigration, digestion.
Nor is the issue courage or top form
though both are necessary in order
to play sweep over the borders of official
forms that need be completed and punctuated.
Not nostalgia not horror not righteousness
though in various degrees these are the alarm
clock perched on the wobbly armoire, child
of one Eternity and an enraged grownup
who saw Her bathing one day at the non-
political shore of childhood and caused
them to merge into a murderous
infinity whose issue is fiery death
and more death. For now they are kept apart
by the writing hand: the pen prevents
the closing of the fist and prices being
what they are it's a good thing too.
Not indignation intelligence rage
though in various bourgeois measure
these too once mixed well to steer
the hornet nest of culture causing bees
to rise from pamphlets into better print.
Home is a car on the road to a cottage
filled with storytelling mythmaking rustics
leaning on a future composed of woven pelts,
miles of sausages, milk and approximate figures
which form the antihistorical peak
where one rests in the company

of national fiction at its most formal ease
under a sky of homespun ambiguities and goat.
No those are not the issues though each line
makes the jar buzz and sets the fashion free.
The issue is ease, and when. The bitterness
thereof is the lack of it, the Sunday
afternoon going to bad movies
made by people one knows slightly,
then letting the haze of a cigarette
over Turkish coffee push the country
forward, a miraculous machine
that is the opposite of a cement truck.

Casino Pierre

The world goes on quite happily
without being pressured by anything more
than everybody in it.
Celebrate by ball-in-snow,
Aleut game played for fish.
But if it's Spring like now
baseball is best, for Cokes.
After watching for a year
I discerned where the ball was
thereby noting that after watching
for a while it's possible to see.
Playing with players
who spend their life playing
makes players play better
and all I need in order to be
a great player is to play
every day of my life
a program I have followed
religiously like a diet.
Ah, sun you are not a ball
but we just can't help using you that way,
like a baby and a vitamin.
Down the cautious streets
the circumspect century deflates.
Did the rest lose the war
of nerves or are they deeply
bored? Pumped full of holes
by wretched points of print & light.
Their watching is dull
and when they play it's
like rival offices banging
staplers on a square drawn on the floor
of the hall between them exactly
as the water fountain spouts blood.
Much peepee caca seriousness.
Shaving is both normal and welcome.
But there is only so much
of one's own stupidity
that makes sense or amuses
which is why the flesh is meant

and not the floor, or even the arena.
Everybody has to find out
what they were designed for
and though most voters never break
down the box with the secret
instructions, it behooves the great
bumbler to bow a humble head before
the waters we're close to drinking.
Being tolerant is the only revelation
I hope for. In America
everybody's in the electric
chair, the papers' low
voltage chair or TV's electric
high-chair. I never confuse
my inner life with my
secret one. Thus *par exemple* when I cross
myself on the street I don't
wink or say hello or tip
the iceberg in my heart toward
my hat. Fat is the body's
revolt against the rules.
Citizens, voting is not enough.
What hides in the already
enforced and geometrical
is neither safety nor bliss
but a nightmare needing time.
Optimism is the tendency
to underline. Vagueness
is any number of alien eggs.
One-liners are here to correct
your imperfectly understood idea
of what's possible. Spotlights
on the baroque flesh selling arks.
And aphorisms when they make the line,
know that only girls make it better.
They do as if Spring was a given
which it is, in spite of the loud
summer in which the blinded wrap
their terror of the snapping bud
where I keep myself half
sleepy for the next call
from my Vantage Ultra Lights pack.

Roto: How the Bourgeoisie Dream

Human, step not into the Middle
    of the Road!
That's for Trucks!

★

I train the gaze.
Particularly useful center stage.

★

Not arrested *for* pot:
    arrested *by* it.

★

Earbulk.

★

The embarrassment of creation:
    I made *that?*
Certain days in December
the light surrounds me with the circumstances
of my birth.
I'm glad they made *this*.
    Prism jism.

★

All games are games of Yes and No.
The aggressor says Yes.

The defender says No.
Sweet fruits of victory:
    your enthusiastic subjects.
Bitter fruits:
    sore losers, ideological cases.

★

At the end of time
    au bout du temps
psi factors go through,
    cholera & ponies,
thud of great ideas:

I had this advantage
in my mode of life.

★

A green bug
with a white border
on "the book that killed my summer."
I am what you might
call "a beneficial bug."
    I turned,
        walked away.
That butterfly had *legs!*

★

"Famous Places We Had Fights In Front Of"
    $8.95 in paper.
Where were you at those same times,
    O Bald Soprano?

★

Five years is not a long time
    to the steady heart.

★

Mmmmmmm. I want to
    be Taj Mahal!
        Mmmmmm. Candyman!
    It has been long.

★

Rising from the glib
    I become inchoate & inarticulate
        thank God,
& then I shock myself with the truth.

The newspapers
    flap around me
after replacing literature
    but nothing flies.
Woman's body in the foreground
    applies for historical site status:
was once battleground:

263

angels wanted in,
men wanted out,
but now it wants to be commemorated
but I think: Airport!
Certain Indians who live in books
are gathering
about the unaware reader.

He will be eaten in the bookstore.

Intention

for Tom Clark

Poems are be not intended
therefore I be always writin
never intendin

"Wake up/have coffee/
write a poem/what else/
is there" (Elinor Nauen)

Wake up/have coffee/puzzle
dream/about attention:
partial, full & deep./Attention
paths/are fascicles./They work
negatively./We engage only
inattention./So go back/
to sleep/dream some more/
about doors./There is

the temptation to sprinkle
quotation marks about:
(and slashing 'em)
in that sense intention
abounds to make legit
the sense in which attention
could be intentional.

My intention is to make a poem
which includes all the great
lines ever written;

I intend this poem to be here
long after you've gone.

It was my intention to present
you with something
leading to sex. I intended
to apologize for the other night
with this humble poem
which has nothing to do with it.

I intend to sue you for character
defamation, let this poem serve
as a pre-subpoena. Intentionally,
I leave these little scratches
on your desk, I made them in a dream.

Intent upon my feelings I came
upon these words: I was full of good
intentions until I saw what I'd wrought
and swore to nevermore complain. Ill
intentions got me here with the ill
wind of the age filling the sails
of my poem: I'll make you something
on purpose to offset being lost.

It was the intention of all present
to palliate loss with literature:
it all came to naught when our leader
folded up the tent of his splendid
intentions, mounted anybody's steed,
took off in an uncertain direction.

What is found depends entirely
on being lost.

The failure of internationalism
is due in part to its containing
intention; likewise intonation,
internation, installation.

We knew exactly where to install
beauty but the electrical codes
are a century old, so we had
to start from scratch with noble
intentions but not much
enthusiasm which doomed us.

Furthermore, there is enough
intention in language
to sink any would-be orator
so why give headache to yousself,
who are a mess of botched intentions

as it is, Harry?

We considered the proposition
that the body might be
a superbly intentional
cooperative farmed out
to a cosmic purpose
and that the poem in its
organicity might be more
like the body than any-
thing less organized
and came to rest upon
the thought that the poem
like and as a body has no
choice, there being little
in nature or in art that
isn't organized instantly
upon expression: to make
is to order which is why
it is important to make
without a plan. Intention
lands one in bed with cliché,
which is somebody's old plan
to bed somebody else's old
plan—Don Juan's intentions

were from the beginning
to seduce the good ladies
of Seville though he had most
rudimentary ideas on how
to proceed, having only
an attitude and not a system.

Attitude differs from intention:
it is the Ur-ground of action
before the plan. Yes, I have
an attitude but it's no plan,
mother, I just want to set sail
for parts unknown, and later
when we recall the journey
for our homebound friends
we'll invent a whole new journey

we will never have unless we leave
right now, forget the telling.

I never intended to get around
the two things that smack of intention,
the two forbidden rocks upon whose flanks
many a traveler cracked and died:
post-intention and autograph.

Long after the journey's done
the post-intentional revisionist
plunges his Soviet pen into the facts
and spaces them intentionally
to make visible the line
on which flutter the bloody rags
of certain swollen egos.
I have done this, and I'm not proud.

Likewise the autograph by being
set before the journey like the word
journey before mounting,
pollutes the very journey with intention.
Of this I have been also guilty.

Forgive us our intentions, dear reader,
they were only attitudes gone flatter.

Mnemogasoline

Under the tropical moon
the peaceful hooker
discoursed on the Gestalt God
with a cat on her shoulder
slowing the motorists down.
She was without fear
as the small Honda went past
bound for the warfront against auto-amnesia
being waged on the old narrative line of defense.
The Honda stopped and a technical
designer at Disney Studios,
who that very day
had been observed doodling on the job
a thing unrelated to Mickey,
and accused of spying,
got out and advanced toward her.
Rather than apologizing, I quit,
he to her explained.
Go to sleep,
said the peaceful hooker.
She wore white stretch pants
& a red sweatshirt inscribed OPIUM
& she took his hand and laid him
on the steps at Sproul Plaza in Berkeley.
He woke up surrounded by a forest of sleeping bags.
A protest was being held, concerning Apartheid.
It was just before dawn.
The rows of moonlit bodies looked like plaster
tempura dishes in the window of Chez Japan.
The intimate tempura of sleep hid the sushi of youth
& filled the present with the romance of another time,
but inflated slightly like a Hong Kong import.
A lightly spun idea dew plied lightly the multicolored polyester,
leaving a dark trench where the speed of commodification
met the definition of symbolic exchange values,
i.e., the labels were inside out,
overturned by nocturnism.
The technical designer stretched in the last ditch of his youth
& rose to embrace the bagels wafting from the bistros.

On the street that morning at about 8:20 A.M.
an ancient man with Pomo d'Oro hair and a sharp
Mephistophelian moustache
was making a telephone call
from a heavily graffitied booth that had
miraculously preserved a clean Southern pane.
He was calling somewhere very far because his lips
formed a small sorrowful noose
like an egg smashed in at the top by a child during
some ancient Easter, soon to be tossed, child and egg,
into the chute of history whence little returns.
I recognized him: it was the lover
of the last Queen of Romania,
a famous playboy of another era.
When I looked, the ancient lover's face cracked:
I saw apologies sucked out of various moonlights
in countries no longer on the map
& he appeared to say, or rather his face did:
"I didn't sleep with her. Very sorry."
But the pomade in his hair said otherwise.

I opened the door of the café
for the belle holding five iced coffees,
who said: "You read my mind."
"It was writ large," I spoke,
"but I'd like to read your body better."
My speech went unnoticed,
having never truly left my throat until this very moment,
but the ancient playboy behind the wall of graffiti
put his hand over his heart and keeled over,
a vessel of Eros sunk by a phone.
I was the first on the scene
& was reluctant to use the very phone that he...
but I did
& paramedics entered the scene in spattered angel suits.
Unbeknownst to anyone I gave him the lover's salute,
silently before the medics came.

In our mutual country several thousand miles to the east
that mad dictator Ceaușescu, a triple-chinned gargoyle,
whose place in Hell is being kept by toothless political
prisoners fanning the flames with tracts

(he had once succeeded the man who'd overthrown
the queen the dead man loved)
was ordering the demolition of the ancient capital
to make room for statues of himself.
A 16th-century church gave way to a badly executed bronze head.

I notice that the etiquette of gazing in America's cities
has to do with the loss of concentration due to zoning.
The absence or the presence of cafes
is proportioned in direct ratio to gazing eyes.
What looks oblique is really lost
opportunities in real estate.
Other places employ other gazes, terrain-modulated to take in
adventure.

Even the old are only myopically casual:
they too are working for love.
I am tortured by certain looks
I get in dreams from people in my past
who, not content to die and tear a hole in me,
continue staring from beyond.
I find a nervous tropical translation
of those looks in humid cities like New Orleans
or Rio de Janeiro.
In these the dark is moist.
The buildings I would build from the crossings of gazes
by the dead with the living
stand in my mind, blue lines in a blueprint on the immense
glasstop table of a Texas developer.
I would replace the dictator's statues with those.
Besides standing, sheltering, and allowing one to be observed
while seemingly unaware, by one or many,
or to be invisible if one wished,
these buildings would change every hour,
a mix of Persian gardens, Paris cafes, Casbah tents,
Marseille alleys, movable streets, floating flowerbeds,
swaying awnings, and dark dives where to wallow
in the sadness of running out of things to buy.
The passive-poetic of night-day reversal
will enhance the mode of sexy difficulty.
I hope to instill in the construct a feeling
of phones ringing in the steam, and clothes falling

around an ontologically attractive metaphysical node set into the
structure at all levels to make it possible to turn anywhere
one feels the benevolent divine urge of the subject.
What is a subject?
Something that can hold, I expect, for many pages, hours, miles.
Why are your moods so *long?* someone asked me once.
At the time I barely knew the joys
of the heavenly fifth wind,
where you stand straining the membrane
on the back of all things
against the current of time.
But now when I go into the unknown
I like to travel a few miles.
Everywhere is a new city, everything must be seen at once.
There are, of course, *moments*, peaks where
one story is soldered to the next,
narrative ditches where flattened against the seams
old demons crouch waiting for sentiment to let them out.

After I left the scene of the death of the lover from the Old World
I took the Greyhound bus to Baton Rouge.
A cowboy was telling a girl about his dog Skipper
how many times she ran away before she made it
& about the time he was a welder on board a ship
& a dog kept him prisoner all night one night in Panama,
with a black man who told him about another dog
who jumped after someone who went down in a pond somewhere
in a southern region of the United States known as Dogtown, AL,
& she remembers the day her daddy shot her dog
for biting the village doc whose own dog then took an ear off
Chunky, her own mutt—and the bus didn't rock to a stop,
it growled into the nine-dog night
describing a circle that took in the welder, me, the bus,
the years, the blueprints of desire, all surrounded
by a thick circle of dogs.
Don't forget, the former ship welder said,
about the girl killed last night in this morning's newspaper
by a mad dog, "prob'ly a nigger or a kike or sumpthin."
"It don't take much for a kid to disappear,"
says the tattooed girl,
a real history of American bad girlhood on her,
blue arrows through red hearts of link chain.

America's wretched riders are arranged by subject matter.
"Dog." "Tattoo." "TV Guide."
There are no foreign students holding Ameripasses.
The front half of the Dawg packs bibles and guns.
The back half is escapees from institutions,
free-lance murderers, sexual desperadoes,
swamp flowers of genetic damage.
"I left a bible in a motel in Hollywood,
and now they are making a movie from the parts I underlined,"
my bench mate tells me.
I study the tattoos in front of me.
The pictographs testify to the narrative urge.

Later that month in the avant-garde capital of San Francisco
another movie is being shown.
It is black and white.
Many frames tremble. A girl in one of them opens
a chill window, letting in the fog.
In many frames thereafter she opens the window.
There are also upside-down parts in a park.
The girl's knee decked in a deco sock.
A door frame.
The filmmaker explains that he has a birth defect
& that this film essay on love
is proof of a dyslexia from which fountainlike
a plethora of bad decisions have dogged him all his life
until they issued upon the weary frames.
Having committed also lifetimes of them before this life
he sees the sign of healing upon himself in the movement
of the handheld camera, helping him to switch
polarities, so that he might become
that glory of late research, a Left Hander, a South Paw.
To this end, and to hasten its coming,
he does everything with his left,
leaving trails of calligraphed paper
in a childish left hand behind him
in cafes and cinematheques.

I have a mild dyslexia as well.
An inability to distinguish left from right.
I call it organic anarchism.
It saves time.

But the filmmaker always going left
needs constant readjustment, as he can feel megadoses of vitamins
traveling him like beatniks through the world's *inclinations*
which must be *corrected* by utopia or eternal life,
whichever comes first.
His body is defective, he believes, in places
where it is unfocused on by moral chemistry,
just as reality's defective where the shaky lens is shut.
We, organic anarchists, *au contraire*,
see reality's defects precisely in those places
where art's been stepping in and making scenes.
My hometowns, all of them, are sadly now
overrun by artists who are the church keys letting
the tourists out of the sardine cans of the middle class.
Reality's birth defects are magnified by art
until tourists with opera glasses stand
in the pretend infant urine of false representation
looking out into the fake past,
rendered useful to the connoisseur, alas, but lost
to all native sense until retired into a single postcard.
My own childhood town, transformed by reference,
gathers its platonic blueprints into a ball
& rolls into view, there to become a drop containing
a time of pristine transport,
while being, as far as I can tell,
a postcard in the hand of the baffled
tourist who pays dearly for his holograms.
The fake town is redesigned to show even the wear of adoration,
even the places where memory works it over,
tear grooves, canals polished by tongues,
long unsplintered beds dug by stretched index fingers
into the angels pointing at the ceiling of Teutsch Cathedral,
a veritable army of stretched hands and arms.
It would be good
if the shoddy translation job in inferior materials
could stand in contrast to the shining drop in my sometime head.
It's unbelievable how shabby the real Rome is!
Like kept prisoner by a dog on board the working history of the world.
Poetry plies the rift like a bird dog in a Mannerist painting.

"Is Mr. Wisdom here?"
"No but mebbe I can find Mr. Stupid for you."

274

"I am very very sorry to have disturbed you."
"You didn't disturb me. You fucked with my mental *balance!*"

The appropriateness of the locus
of the crime, i.e., "the breaking of the shoe."

Seeing the back of a beautiful girl walking,
I can feel her with my whole body. Amazing.
I must prevent her from turning. It becomes my job.
Maybe she's not a girl at all, but a mailbox, or a newsstand.
Walking behind her down Telegraph Avenue, this lovely Sunday morn,
I wonder if sex is the opposite of schizo-
phrenia.
Finding myself philosophizing behind her
easy-swinging lovely back, I think to overcome her
and to ask, "Is sex the opposite of schizo-
phrenia?"—
when she turns around,
& smiles at me directly slicing me in half:
"How are you this gorgeous day?"
"Yourself?" I say astonished and inaudible,
meaning her Self as different from her back
which I somehow feel "I know," that it is "mine."
"Oh fine," she says, meaning her back too.
She touches the red frame of my glasses:
"It feels good," she says,
"to take a break from the Eros seminar."

Electromagnetic field reader & manipulator
just inside the gates of my head, shakes his head.
Ah yes the fields exist and they are knowable.
There is nothing bigger than them: not even Time.
But there's a rub: Timing.
I'm on my way to the airport and she's one day late.
The timing of knowledge is the crux.
But in her crux time is made right.
The crux is always present to the crucial.
Mistimed knowledge lines the pits
the true originals lie in becoming drops.
But there was never a time when things could have been different.
They are always different.
Does uselessness invalidate seeing?

275

Should schizos be protected like brujos or restored like vases?
In the sexualized field, analysis (chemistry) encounters action (faith)
for purposes of reassessing the description.
The tearing of the veils,
the breaking of the crust,
are immediately followed by the blinding
revelation of organic
complexity underneath.
To make another whole it is necessary to remake all the parts.
Which are themselves wholes formed of further particulars.
There is no self-generated
return to the surface
because there is no "self."
The fragmented cluster of particulars
in a state of rapid disintegration
whirls by in a search of a matching cluster
& is further pulled apart.
Violence from the outside has certain advantages
if the object to be put
back together
serves some function in that state.
Should I now fall apart
I am doubtful if enough
usefulness could be found in me—
barring discovery of the drops—
to justify
bringing me back to one unit.
Better to mark each part with the word *Taboo*.
But if you're sexy enough they'll name a perfume after you.

At the truck stop where America's last free storks nest,
a killer leaves a Popeye's chicken box.
Inside it is the hand of formerly his best friend.
The former welder on the bus retches and smokes dust.
The ship's cook once made nail clipping soup.
For one hundred bucks Greyhound is good forever.
"We haven't been off the bus for eight years,
except to buy Popeye's." Sunsets, sunrises,
nausea-lined faces form solidly into a coffin bashing
rudderless against the TV.
We on the other side let's wave at the lumpenproletariat.
Sooner will sulfates cyanide silicon selenium salt

276

go through the eye than minor psychos into America.
Who remembers Juan Corona?
Gacy?
Whitman of Texas?
Ng and the Chowchilla boys?
Where is the handsome Black Doodler
with his sketches of soon-to-die lovers?
The Zodiac Killer who scratched his stars on corpses?
Charles Manson of the Beatle-mysteriumed Bacchae?
Williams of Atlanta, bridges, strangled children, night?
Where are the newspapers of yore?
The ship of gore?
Scuzz, scum, flotsam, dusted, juiced, sick,
the Dark goes Greyhound and Big Red, and hitches
toward the TV glass.
Wave harder now.
There used to be a way through the glass,
some of the old-timers remember.
You could hitch a ride through literachoor.
Why, there was Kerouac.
You could go through him right up to America
& it was like you'd always been there.
Well, half in and half outta da glass at least.
There used be a mesh of coincidence right about here,
& conjecture, riding the narrative folds to some under-
standing of Eros in liberty, and then it was a short hike
home.
I'm looking, but for what?
It's been mended.
There is a preacher in the hole collecting a junk army:

Hallelujah brothers & Hosanna!
It was a dark hour when they put him in the grave.
It was Friday!
But Sunday is here!
They don't celebrate Easter in Poland today like we do
They have the jackboot on their neck!
It's Friday in Poland!
But Sunday is coming!
The Soviets are strafing villages in Afghanistan
Killing women & children
It's Friday in Afghanistan!

But Sunday is coming!
And Napoleon was broken at Waterloo
Where he kept hitting and hitting
But Wellington's line wouldn't break!
Two thousand years ago Satan threw everything he had at Jesus
But the rock didn't break!
And today godless Communism throws everything against
the rock of faith & the rock doesn't break!
And the media knows not an iota of the Gospels!
One day is coming when you'll turn on your TV & only the voice
of the Gospels be coming through!
It's Friday in the world
But Sunday is coming!

The drama of Eros and Self goes on in the pews
where the cross-eyed folk wink at each other.

Back in Berkeley, California, I am given a starring role
In the Opéra Bouffe of Exile!
A million forgotten ideas fight for my ear.
I sing the part of the Ear.
My fellow wanderers want my ear.
No, no, I say what you want is America's Eye!
But they are all stubborn like my mother.
"Since she became a cyclops, we had no rest, your mother and I..."
There are ministers without portfolios singeing their barbered
whiskers on a violence without victims...
Academics without chairs, desks, carrels, universities...
Monarchists without a king tripping on the red carpet of the
hotel lobby with vials of blood in their palsied pockets
from which they furtively sip as their wrinkles briefly
disappear...
Fascists without leaders, fuehrerless fanatics...
Nudists dressed in the armor of discarded truths...
Icon painters falling to their knees with heavy wooden crosses
about their meaty necks...
The very lover of Queen Marie who has reappeared with his
plasterboard
hair wandering all over the map of our vanished country,
carving new valleys of Vitalis broadcasting yellowed
instructions and codes carrying from phone booth to phone
booth that sickle-thin fin-de-siècle smile

that says always, forever, I didn't really, besides
it wasn't any good, it was a literary idea, she was
a writer you know ...
but no book will ever be about us?
I see ideologues of splinters of splinters
arranged in tiers, a political cake of parties
on frayed tablecloths in unrestored European hotels
waiting for the beringed fingers of a native autocracy
to plunge through the icing for a taste of their hearts.
Arranged arachnid-style around the chandeliers
are painters of icons "in the traditional manner"
waiting for a signal to descend upon the cake flames
which are tall Orthodox silver crosses
shaking aromatic powder or the dust of the IXth Arrondissement.
They have traveled long distances to praise God,
& have some cake, have some cake.
God is everywhere an occasion for a gâteau-da-fé.
But perhaps they all wait for muscle, not for religion.
For young punks to back up the bitter yeast of their spectacular
escapes from everywhere into the story
no one wants to hear, alas. Like tremulous
and not-so-young mademoiselles from another century,
refined beyond present-day understanding,
they speak 25 languages & not one of them the vulgate.
The hotel's tarnished gilded salon trembles during the verse-recitation
of the boring epic,
wishing it was listening to Charles Baudelaire instead.
Everything désuet & lost is in the dusty escritoires,
shorted violetas, misclustered chandeliers.
I meet a young woman here. In the shade of her violent eye makeup
are her recent memories when with 13 of her friends
she lay in front of the President's limousine,
her hi-heeled shoes pointing an ultimatum at the spiky
tyrant in his Brooks Brothers blazer & Calvin Klein jeans,
as her high-placed family trembled awaiting the phonecall
from the secret police.
In my day a certain gentleness still attached to the electrodes,
a multithreaded rag of innuendoes especially licensed
by one's lycée to pass themselves off as metaphors.
Brutality hadn't quite become art for art's sake.
I meet a great critic.
After 5 years in prison,

he is only interested in California boys.
They say, he tells me, that this is the capital
of perverted sex! I am a FEROCIOUS pervert!
They have diseases here,
an alarmed dissident folklorist tells him.
They might catch something from *me*, shouts the critic,
& the pathos of lost diseases shines briefly
in cot B of his former cell,
political, historical, intellectual diseases that flare
in his joints and at the seams of the world's wounds giving
the critic's eyes a certain flaming luster.
What is a virus to those?
Places where folk die of philosophy
don't share geography with places where people die of diseases.
They share no air, no words, no maps.
Three to a room, they're kept
waiting for people to enter & tear
apart in interesting patterns.
I am conversing with the chief ex-spook from America's
Secret Radio Police who is about to break the news
to me that I make a lousy Ear
when the lobby fills suddenly with humans in wheelchairs,
torsos on skateboards,
arms in slings,
steel hooks,
bandanas over deep body holes.
The chief says, "Here is the next convention,
they booked them one day early, there will be a mess."
Exile has its internal tourist attractions and a timetable out of whack.
Mistimed etc lines the pits etc.
I watch my countrymen carrying an unfair argument with the ghosts
trapped in their memory drops, and I wish
I could rain on them to take them home.
The old country and their youth are intact in the blue atmosphere
around each and every one of them,
& they are ready to die for it.
Some would do double duty and also die for art.
I stand astonished at the certainty of what art.
A bouquet of little indulgences waits crammed in the jewel box
of my memory to be pried ajar by my fellow exiles.
I enter the escritoire of meta-finances, filled to the transoms
with hotel bills and laundry tickets,

& look at the many cities below
unchanged in the geography of desire:
Vienna, Buenos Aires, Tangiers, Paris, London, New York and Caracas.
They are my mantilla's arousal, my calling card,
this premier assent of cities of exile into the heart
of my explicative genius at its flood-season height.
A drop would suffice to render understanding unto all
but the operation is not visual, not designed for a flat Eros,
though it is a little shabby
like Spain maybe before the Conquest.
What can't be had is worth equipping an armada for.
What is invisible always has a door.
A solid brass door encrusted hopefully with the eyes of romance.
It's Berkeley, Brazil, Lima, Bangkok, or France.
The esprit of despair takes poets by the throat to produce
not a Classical Age but a holding pattern, a sterling fork
to tune the streets for better holding forth.
I am breathing through one hundred straws,
each one designed to suck in another *paysage*
& I am bleeding through eight hundred little wounds
each one mined by an expatriate's *vernissage*
which is why when they hold me at a certain angle like an ear,
in the sun, I am a copper sieve sifting red flour on
piles of little uncirculated shiny coins labeled *Mnemogasoline Drops.*
Royalties on the books that result thereof are paid by the wind,
alone among the elements to read.
The whirring of iridescent scholarly beetles bores the light.
I did set out to be an icon, it's true.
The people in my village wished fervently for it,
even though I was born in a rather large city,
& always had the lowest opinion of hicks—even when,
I shamefully confess, the Lord lowered his rifle on the peasants
& had them made first into dust, then into symbols.
I became a sort of icon I called The Sword and the Mascara.
There are no watchers, of course, and this is good.
It would be fine if there were watchers who knew that the watched
were hiding something even if it was only their artificiality
which made them act that way.
Which way is that?

The victims of art are now simply called citizens.
They display their victimization

like a passport to civilization.
Their formal bodies are art. I mean, mine is.
We stand between the books and cannot be told apart.
If we are picked up we open everywhere and can be read quickly.
We stand in galleries mournfully unable to look as modern as that.
We walk out of the pages of books and back on the streets
lined with epochal reminder craft just like the entries we mean
to stay in when our bodies go.
We are enticing but there aren't any observers.
Who can stand outside to say Ah?

The problem with autobiography
is that you find yourself in places already written up.
The world takes on an insufferable literary air.
Everybody's in it & they are always home.
There is a volume of déjà vu.
Even if you have changed things ever so slightly.
The déjà vu is distorted ever so literally,
reality takes on that defective air,
a defect of translation passing for a defect of birth.
The shadows of the defective turn on their hinges,
tarnished by reference to adoration & translation.
Say what? Say what? Repetition is not exact?
Hence realism's impossible?
The world believes in sex, the absurd and gymnastics,
& I *could* to keep it at that,
but even with my back to the beautiful girl I can still
plot her abduction from fertile mythos
in inexact replication of every situation.
"Beautiful back, beautiful, sinuous, grace-driven back,
with only primitive political ideas,
a great curved organ for paradox, called 'spine,'
I'm going to caress you with my breath, in time with your fifth
unliterary sense, with my rainbow brush!"
I would not mind being leaned against your back and shot!
Viva To All That!
Believe me, I would. The fields are real, they are knowable, they
exist, there is nothing bigger than them,
not even our two human bosses: Mister Time & Comrade Timing.
It is not as a poet I speak but as a pedestrian & a boy.
People, love your waitresses and your bus drivers,
& the veins that run from the back of the bus

282

where the crazies retch,
to the front where the depressed
think everything is their fault,
& the paranoiacs
that nothing is.
Oh, sad is their song!

Y Un Canción Por E.

We are elements of design just now.
We can't decide between food or love.
This is such thick book I fear
it will take years to read.
Don't got it. Fresh out.
A week? Don't got that neither.
A day? A night? Too long.
An hour then? A minute?
OK, but you must hurry.
Close the book. Let's
Run. Jump over the fat Turk
scarfing up the van.
Put your face in mine,
roll up your skin in mine,
saves space as well as time,
don't get tangled
in the tugboat lines,
they're there for other crimes.
Cut across fields,
streak through alleys, go
over the national defenses
of several small
nations. Like that.
And you who hold the soap bubble
between your chopsticks
over us like an umbrella
over two sick mammals
see that what quivers under
is merely animation
to throw into relief
what rages above,
cheek, eyes, lips, etc. Oh love.
Has watching hit a snag,
is everybody's watch
broke or in decline?
Quite fine thank you,
having a life.
I didn't say intriguing,
I said weird. And all.

Christmas in New York

for Laura

Trees torpedoes Soviet galoshes
books violins woolen socks
Mexico Argentina Korea Peru.
We promenade in steamy human corn.
An actress with her arm wrapped
around gift-wrapped mannequin
calls mom in snowbound Arkansas.
People people the island
wrapped around each other
lit scroll-like Chinese on
Chinatown marquee
where we suck duck feet
that once walked the sturdy earth.
Oh tender feet whose flesh we sweetly suck!
The string on our hearts is nigh undone.
Ghosts nine feet tall come bounding through the slush!
We are so nicely dressed!
Parcels with wings in ghostly disarray
argue with their lost souls in traffic
gifts exchanged desperately fast!
We tangle ourselves to wind-whipped
humanity blowing about the future
when our children will have nice toys.
The world has a million elbows
resting on fine tables in the bistro de la vida.
All exchange is slush balderdash
o great haberdasher!
O pure metal money.
O truth under duress—this being
that time—there are no words
that are not for sale. Yet we know:
outside the body begins the lie.
Outside that the newspaper.
And the bum wrapped in it
will not change tomorrow's news
though tomorrow both paper and body
will be a white mound of snow,
an unsystematic library, confusion

of what lived and what died
before it could be re-read
or how from inside ourselves
the big snow came
to invade with beauty
so recently rent a world.
The magic lounges wrapped
in jukebox steam
give good detail to whatever makes it in.
O baby, call in the surface-to-air messenger,
the caffeinated pigeon
with the beating of his trained
telegraph across the *années.*
O differentiated lumps of *amore!*
O garbage dump masses having us for dinner
you on a platter me on a cloud!
Food for everybody.
L'âme de Madame is now served.
Erectile tissue paper in crêpe de chine
rose-pinks to burst its mauve bows.
Death to the military metaphors:
sentences, captains, bullets, reports.
Without a roof we revel in being,
wrapped for others—keepsakes
of a state and time when
human beings are:

1) rubber animals who bend well and far
        held tightly between frozen mitts

2) empty drawings on swirling imagoes to make credible thickness
        i.e., belabored snowmen and snowwomen

3) impressions on Japanese screen

4) comic algebra

5) excess food covered by tweed

6) mute newlyweds wrapped in a single fur

7) baby mimes doing stuff with their toes

8) company representatives (the Trans-
Siberian Railroad, the Alaska goldrush)

9) travel dust from luminous hair
of aliens with cuneiform legs
dancing the poignant resiliency of almost anything

10) hardy gossamer.

The juke pivots in the end-century
for Genghis wherever he is,
and Elvis Kahn, tailor to history,
in Jersey over the smoke where he
cuts the falling snow to fit
everyone so they'll look sublime:
newts en masque, popes en croûte,
flares on restaurant tables
where the dons of beauty &
donnas of grace pose
in the unfathomable
instrumentation of seated self.
The Dream of Perfection neatly fits
the Dream of Wickedness about the waist
of the Dream of Power round the testes
of the Dream of Transformation.
Above the wingèd tedium
of phones ringing in Christmas splendor
the party calls us to the source
of the objective world
whose diamond opens briefly
like a disco at some pink odd point
where commerce ceases and exchange begins
& dreaming well accoutred
in pleasure and so dry.

A Leafy Angel

to the Columns Hotel

Quietly at the corner table
where the dry fountain
drowns in unswept leaves
under its disconsolate angel,
the slim boy in the shadow
of the blooming jeune fille
has opened Postmodern Art,
a book. Twixt happiness
and unhappiness
the only break we get
she thinks is sleep.
Certain mental interiors
exist only in French
is what he thinks.
Stranger still she is chief thespian
in a play
taking place presently in her mind
where she does bad things
in order to build capital
for masturbation
with a visiting European
on whose shoulders
run little trains
powered by oblivion.
At the streetcar stop
an old woman in mourning black
watches her younger self run
alongside a mostly naked runner
following the streetcar line
to a perfect body.
They are Jasmine and Sweet Olive,
they have just met
in 1924 in The City
That Lives for Its Belles,
a bar.
Stranger, sit quietly here
this evening
at the Columns Hotel

on the terrace at dusk
where light goes out with flair
on froufrou and history.
Outside the body, happily,
begins the lie.

Not a Pot to Piss In

MY LIFE AS A POT

In giving me a subject as big as the world
the distinguished organizers
showed a lot of faith—
as much faith as mud can have in mud—
Given the vastness and the nature
of the subject prose is wholly inadequate
being both square and utilitarian—
this art I decided will only be served by poetry
which is no simple repository
but rather like a shapely pot itself a wholly
surprising recasting of the matter—
Much like human beings themselves, of course,
who were fashioned by god
to store his thoughts in.
God's scattered thoughts were a constant source
of confusion to him
until he conceived of two faithful mugs
that would be a perfect metaphor for his job
which was filling the emptiness.
On the other hand god may have just been playing
and had no need of either metaphors or storage
or frames for his thoughts—
Metaphors and storage may have been the problem
of his playthings—
his playthings having come into being
experienced an anxiety of definition:
what are we and what are we for, they cried,
soon after being shaped,
and hearing no answer, provided themselves
with metaphors, raison d'êtres and other uses.
I like to think that ontological anxiety is the exclusive
property of the created, that the maker has none.
And of course I may be wrong.
We do seem to be made by anxious gods sometimes.

When I was young and didn't have a pot to piss in
I thought a lot about god.
In my cups often my cup overfloweth with god
and I was full of inspiration.

Human life from chamber pot to funeral urn
is a ceaseless pouring from one vessel into another,
I reasoned, so *enivrez-vous* as
Baudelaire said, and when I was perfectly drunk
I was in paradise like a happy jug.

For most of the time in paradise
the primero living pots
had no need of other pots
because rivers flowed directly
into their mouths and whenever they looked up
something delicious and ripe fell for them to eat—
they were perfect self-referential pots
required only to believe in their own self-replenishing
    sufficiency and in the skill of the demiurge—
but then something got into them
    —probably the unsettling thought that they were a metaphor—
and they tried to make pots on the sly while god was sleeping—
they snuck into the shed and started fooling around with his
    cosmic wheel—
and god smashed them to the earth and they were broken into
    shards—
whose history we never stop trying to piece together
    out of the shards we ourselves have left behind—
    millions of shards because since the Fall
    we've had to ceaselessly keep
    making pots to store our food, eat and drink from,
        and write our stories on.

But this god didn't stop there.
He forbade the making of idols as well
and outlawed any object that wasn't plain and functional
such as fat goats, nard boxes, seductive vials and dolls—
so that there was no more arguing with this god
about ceramic art—
and all ceramicists henceforth became pagans.
And as for humans themselves
he imprisoned them forever
in their original forms
so that we are all djinns and djinnies in the jugs
of our flesh waiting for death to let us out.
When I was young I thought a lot about history

and about women
and when my cup overflowed
I often conversed with the djinnie in the jug
& she obliged me with a parade of vessels of eros
from the mysteries of all religions
from Semiramis to Delphi
a profusion of Lilliths and Venuses
whose cornucopic flow made me giddy & amorous.
It was a wholly different creation I saw under their spell.
In this one after god fashioned
woman from the mud
he had just enough left over to make her a pet.
So he made her a boy poet.

Not so—an older & wiser drinkard told me.
After god made man and woman
he blew life—or faith—into the man
and then tired went to put more fire into his breath
leaving the dog in charge of the urn that was
going to be woman
and the devil came up and asked the dog:
Please dog please can I play with this form?
I'll give you a fur coat if you let me play with this form.
OK, said the dog, and the devil played with the form
and put ninety moods in her.
When god came back he was mad:
Because you let the devil play with my form, dog,
you will wear your coat forever even in summer.
And that was one hot dog from then on.

Well, then, I told the older drinkard,
I propose to you that if god was the first potter
the devil was the first artist
and the dog the first buyer, admirer, gawker and fool.
And as for woman and her moods
they continue to produce the metaphors
as well as the actual objects
we slog through history with,
objects which festoon even the bible like a museum
from the wedding at Cana to the platter holding John's head,
in spite of god's express command against playing with mud
    or fire or yourself—

a Pandora's box full of dishes, cups, jugs, pitchers and urns
on which are carved the bodies & faces of people past & present
   whose fingers shaped them, and left their mark—
And this bounty, this cornucopia, this generative
   formal imagination is the reason why we eventually survived,
spilling out of the disappointment of losing paradise into an
   eros of our own celebrated by daily ware
   as well as by ceremonial clay—

And of course by now it was much later
not only in history but in the night
and I would have given all the empty cups
piled between us on the table like a tomb
for a girl or woman with a living womb.

When I got home I fumbled with the key
in the moonlight that barely lit the ancient keyhole
of our Saxon house in Transylvania.
Shining from the glass case which mother kept
under a different lock and key
were seven plates from mother's village
in the mountains, and a cheap porcelain Napoleon
she had picked up at some Austrian fair.
The patterns on the dishes could also be found
in the embroidery of certain dresses at the back
of her closet which stood there mysteriously alert.
About the plates I knew only that they were meant
for special days that had not yet arrived
in my lifetime. A wedding perhaps. Mine? Hers?
A feast so grand the whole apartment block would come.
All our neighbors, former peasants mostly, had been
forced by misery and decrees to move into the city,
and they all displayed in cases similar to ours
the plates of their villages, mysterious discs inscribed
with the signs of their particularity, the lost
co-ordinates of lives that had once been round and cosmic
and revolved like saucers about the saucers and the plates
of their specific differences. They were maps these plates
of lives once lived in cyclical ease, maps of a handmade world
that knew the wherefores of its food and celebrated
its making and its transformation in the proper ware.
These dishes waited for their weddings now

in cement cubicles hived about the steel industries
of our town. One day, I told myself, you'll get
to set them all in their full splendour on the tables
covered with handmade lace and linens. It will be
the wedding of the sun with the moon, and all the stars
will stand there burning patterns as they eat.
But no such day. My mother had by now relegated
these dishes to the status of display and she had
for the most part forgotten their provenance, and their
meaning. She placed them on the same plane as her cheap
Napoleon, and was mighty ticked that morning when
she found him smashed into a hundred bits, even his hand
which he kept so carefully in his coat. It appears
that in my drunken glory I had climbed up on the case
and holding him in my hand I had made a speech about
the loss of our selves and our roots in jumbled signs
and when I was done I hurled him to the floor.
That much for the glory of reflected lore.

The Saxons who founded Hermannstadt were craftsmen.
The Bruckenthal Museum was full of ceramics & terrors,
    Laocoön was forever strangled by faïence snakes
    & there were snakes curled on plates & bemused fish
    stretching their scales between centuries from Holland
        to Transylvania, and monsters perched above tureens
    who had travelled from Vienna after devouring their diners,
    & scenes of China and Japan patiently waiting for their victims
        to be done eating
        & Greek oil jars in which thieves had slowly dissolved—
    & it was no safer outside the museum where Ilse
    the fräulein who took care of me when mother worked
    took me to her Black Forest house with the ceramic
    German stove for cooking children in the middle of her
        bedroom—When I was asleep she put two hot bricks
        at my feet & roasted me as her porcelain dolls shrieked—
In those days under every bed
was an enormous chamber pot held down by angels
in which lived a fin-de-siècle monster filled with children's
    brains—And all these things were glazed & shiny & full of
    history.
In a country where there weren't many things
where the material world was both thin & threadbare—

you could easily see the light shining through it—
we loved & feared our chamber pots and stoves fiercely
even as we could not remember what was written on them.
But things were certainly written on them
and those few of us who knew how to read read them
without surcease. Ilse, for instance, read Gothic script
to me in the Bruckenthal, intoning Mittel Deutsch like a Latin
   mass—
And now & then in the chiaroscuro of the Bruckenthal which was
   saving money on lights I would encounter an old scholar
   named Ferenc Pasperger who always made notes & wore a coat
   so shiny & so thin you could see his yellow parchment skin
   underneath. One afternoon he bid me put my ear to the bulge
   of a pot that was quite a bit taller than me
   & had grooves on its fat belly. "Listen!" he said. I listened.
I heard something like a far-off sea something I'd heard before
   in seashells. I told him so. "No, listen deeper!" he said,
   and as I did it seemed to me that I heard voices talking,
   shouting, laughing at some great distance, behind a wall.
I heard children. "That's it! That's it!" said Ferenc, his bony
   forehead close to mine. "Those are," he said, "the voices
   of the people who made this pot, and you can hear their
   children talking, and whoever was around just then."
It was true. I listened most of that afternoon and heard people
   long dead conversing in the pot.
Ferenc thought that the grooves were like grooves on a record
   and that the makers of pots used their tools to record
   their worlds, and that we could hear them if we listened.
And that fired my imagination & I thought that I could listen
   to Socrates, for instance, if only I found the right pot
   because he hung out in the market around the pot makers
   & the mob, or to anyone for that matter, and that I could
   pick up secrets whispered within range of the turning stylus:
   hints of hidden treasure, plots to kill, the mumbled seeds
   of conversation that became *Gilgamesh*, or *Don Quixote* or
   The Last Testament of François Villon—
And ever since then I've been listening. I put my ear to the old
   pots and hear the vanished people gab. And sometimes I pick
   them up, the great and the not so great dead I steal
   my verses from—

Hidden on dishes, pots and sculptures in plain sight
is our history and our peculiar rhythms—

I also found a little later—
I was growing up fast in those days—
that in the old cemetery
among the amputated angels and the listing urns
were ideal places to hide with a girl.
I hid there with Aurelia.
One summer afternoon she and I lay on the bodies
of two knights carved with their arms crossed
on their tombstones
who made a low sorrowful moan of long gone love
until we tumbled between them and there on the broken
debris we commenced the old dance.
Many times the startled angels sighed and fell
off their pedestals while the urns tipped as our hot
fire passed through them.
And then it rained & you could hear the dead
straining to leave the squishy slimy squeaky mud
and to burst their bonds of crumbling stone
as we continued
working the clay and the shards with our bodies
until it was time to go home and catch hell—
those days were full of cracked & babbling ceramics,
urns, jugs & broken pillars to hide behind—
we were like statues or dolls ourselves:
still when the adults were watching
& animated & full of an insane music when they were not.

Having decided to be a poet for reasons having to do
partly with all the whispering text about me
and partly because I was full like a jug with
all the milk of my adolescence
I began putting words on paper
though only incidentally on paper—
I would have liked to write on clay tablets.
Failing that I would
have liked to inscribe the bowls
we slurped our gruel from so that in getting to the bottom
the startled glutton would be confronted suddenly
with his own mortality: "He who made this bowl

salutes you. From now on you are his. Obey his oracle,
you greedy dog!" Or: "You've gotten to the bottom. From
here on out only the journey matters."
In the fifties Communism achieved a Zen-like simplicity.
It was every man and his bowl.
And it was every woman and her single potato
or, on holidays, a bone.
Books were even scarcer.
The only things to read were signs from the past.
And these were written on dishes kept under lock and key.
And on small things that fell on us in the cemetery
from the toppled funeraria: old coins, spiders, withered hearts,
dried livers and coarse spiny flowers.

Consequently, our imaginations were free to spin.
We spun imaginary beings which
unlike the flesh ones are always spun not born.
We were all mind potters turning the wheels of our
blooming flesh into a void made cold by ideology.
And it was a muddy world too because as soon
as you left the dimly lit city with her cracked pavements
and her crackling, sighing and swaying cemetery
you were back in the stew-thick dark of peasant villages
yoked to skinny nags and sluggish oxen
whose job was not to pull these villages anywhere
into, let's say, the 20th century
but to keep them anchored rather
to the Carpathian mountains—
They groaned there at the heart
of dismembered feudal estates,
shadowed by monasteries and castles perched on crags—
in one of these at Arges
a young girl had been built alive into the wall
so that the wall would stand—
and in another Countess Bathory drank
the blood of 650 virgin girls
in order to keep her youth—
and ghosts were still drinking from stone cups
a substance that could have been time itself—
they did not care about communism
they looked rather into a farther past
for that single object, the Grail, and its connection

to god, or some god, or some essential magic.

It can be argued of course that the Grail was itself
capitalism, that its function was to transform the creative
blood or sweat of the divine into the multitude
of objects that fill the world now. The alchemists'
alembics, grinders, mortars, pestles and jars, moved
steadily toward the generative heart of matter where
the pure transformative operation percolated in its sealed
container. Not far from us, in Prague, a rabbi
made a man of clay called a Golem and gave him life
by writing the name of god on his forehead, and when
this lyric statuette began behaving badly the rabbi
did to him what god did to us. He erased the word
and the creature crumbled.

Communism was a golem by the mid-sixties.
It awaited only the hand to erase the word.
God had pretty much been done away with by then
both in the East and the West.
After a time the unsettled creation
that had issued from the lord's kilns
came to the rather
chilling conclusion
that only the murder of god could
restore it to paradise. This conclusion, I must add, was
chilling but inevitable, given the magnitude of our loss
and the grudge we carried ever since we were hurled
like cheap Napoleons from our golden-pot selves into
the muck of history,
the story of which we have scratched into every
available surface
and would have continued to do so to this day
had history not ended & the electronic media
taken its place.
But that's another story.
In the intervening centuries
between the Fall & the deicide
we elaborated our revenge—
by the middle of the 19th we had it—
we did to god what he did to us—
we pulled god out of the heavens

298

and when he fell he too broke into a thousand shards—
that's why there are so many god-struck people now.
This was but simple justice though it is nice that we observed
    the forms
and had Nietzsche sign the official death certificate.
These god-struck people walking about with god-shards
    imbedded in their brains
amble about in large numbers
    while the larger shards
float above their heads and are called flying saucers
    and in this form are seen daily by millions
in the sky and the popular press—
    Though it could also be the case
that some of these saucers were made by ceramicists
    in California & loosed upon the rest of us.
                    (You know who you are!)

The 19th century happened for me around my 19th year.

It is not coincidental that both the 19th century
    and my 19th year
were the sites of an overwhelming profusion of dishes,
pots and soup tureens, broken gravestone angels,
leaf-stuffed gargoyles trying to cough them out,
clay-born worlds
that multiplied in panic and in response
to chimney stacks and factories—
the Victorian world was making a last stand for the handmade
craft in the kitchens and the boudoirs
which gave birth to Freud—
while out of the smoking chimneys of mass-production
Karl Marx was born—
and as for me I was considering marrying Aurelia the girl
from my hometown whose dowry
consisted of one hundred plates
displaying Minoan-like fertility charms
ancient designs that came from Minos via Illyria to Dacia Felix
two marble jars that looked Cretan,
a serpentine goblet that could have been used in Babylonia,
and two hundred black bowls with a red glaze
matched by two hundred cups
with a snake beneath each handle—

an incredible wealth that had come unbroken
through her mountain-folk who had traded
sheep for centuries in the Black Sea–Mediterranean world
where eventually the amphoras of Greece, Rome and Byzantium
encountered the spice jars, oil jugs and wine goblets of the
    Orient, including those huge Arabian Nights pots where Ali
    Baba and the forty thieves hid—

even as the rest of her mother's culture lay in shards
all about her—
her mother worked in a textile factory.
In the end it was all for the best.
We would not have gotten along
and all those dishes would have doubtless
broken on the shoals of our stormy relationship.

I took my writing tablets elsewhere then—
to the West
to a world of happy plastic
a universe of Melmac
nylon, vinyl lounge chairs,
naugah interiors and lava lamps
where the products of ersatz Freud
reclined sipping chemicals
through plastic straws
from tall mass-produced goblets.
This was the Dow Country
the country of Dow Chemicals and napalm.

Thank god for the hippies.
And for Latin America.
In potter sheds inside a secret nation
the children of the plastic people
were making another world
out of clay.
In California I lived with several potters
who made self-refilling coffee mugs, bottomless
    bean pots, self-cleaning ashtrays & vanishing tea cups
that imparted to the tea-drinkers an uncanny Japanese style
    kind of peace that after surpassing all understanding
    led to some fabulous Kabuki-like theatre & sex.
And when my friends talked about their pots it always sounded

to me as if they were talking about sex:
they said wide shoulders, thickened mouth rim, cobalt
   blue under the glaze, long neck, undulating rim, deeply
   recessed, high flaring foot, and once there was
   buff stoneware covered with a white slip. That one
   really got me.
And I could see how one could fall in love with a pot as if it
   were a person & many of my friends
were in fact in love with pots who were a lot less damaged
   than the human fauna that spinned about the place.
And my wife Alice had a dream about a village clustered around
   a pyramid atop which wise elders sat smoking and chatting
and she spent the next year making it: a multitude of villagers
   engaged in tasks about the wells and the fields, women cooking
   children dancing in a circle, people staring out the windows
   & in the middle of it was the pyramid and the elders &
   she called this The Clay People's Republic &
   when she finished it I had a dream that all the people
   who ever lived were now here again made out of clay
   awaiting only a signal to start going about their business
   & I woke up wondering how we would all fit
   on the same earth which is getting smaller as I speak—
In Mexico just across the way
a myriad of gods, goddesses and fetishes
also came out of the ground
and out of kilns
in a jumble of archeology & modernity
pre-columbian past below
insurgent new muralista colors above.
I saw a terra-cotta dog with a human mask
made in Colima
a native hairless dog
and a clay model of an Aztec ball court
with eager spectators
and countless males and females holding
things that looked like rockets—
and clay masks
and priests, shamans, nobles and peasants,
whole worlds, friendly and unfriendly,
representing the seen and the unseen—

but most of all I saw myself

seated at a stall in a plaza of the New World
writing letters for hire for illiterate lovers
while underneath my papers was a stone tablet
on which the writing I did on paper
inscribed itself simultaneously in a cuneiform-type language
that only few could read.
And I became quite the fetishist as you can see.
And in 1989 communism collapsed,
the word gone from its forehead.
The borders of the empires blurred.
The clays across official borders
became visible, an intermingling
that could be fertile & rich.
But simultaneously the pots of small nations
rose from their buried hovels full
of the unsettled honey of a thousand lost wars.
These drums of tightly packed sentiment & hate
are now being carried on the shoulders of hungry mobs
who want them opened, worshipped and divined.
How we break them open without destroying their beauty
or mocking their pain
is the challenge of our art—

My friends, potters digging up the earth,
leaving holes in it until the whole mass of it
becomes artifact or art
you must divine the vectors of its new order—
that's the price for not keeping still in paradise.

After words ceramics are the most legible writing
and words themselves are written mostly upon the dishes
to which I keep my ear,
and what they say is,
it's a long story of mud & of hands
and the hands that fashion the mud refashion the world—
when little hands play in the clay
they make monsters and warriors who pummel each other
who have names & things to say to each other
and twirling ballerinas and princesses who also
have names & things to say to each other
& in play all return to childhood

even self-intoxicated adolescents in their cups
who think a lot about god

that poor god without a pot to piss in
whose shards are now everywhere to be found

Printed in September 1996 in Santa Barbara
& Ann Arbor for the Black Sparrow Press by
Mackintosh Typography & Edwards Brothers Inc.
Text set in Bembo by Words Worth.
Design by Barbara Martin.
This edition is published in paper wrappers;
there are 200 hardcover trade copies;
100 hardcover copies have been numbered & signed
by the author; & 20 copies lettered A to T
have been handbound in boards by Earle Gray
& are signed by the author.

PHOTO: Susan Daboll

ANDREI CODRESCU was born in Sibiu, Romania in 1946. Since emigrating to the U.S. in 1966, he has published poetry, memoirs, fiction, and essays. He is a regular commentator on National Public Radio, and has written and starred in the award-winning movie, *Road Scholar*. His novel, *The Blood Countess* (Simon & Schuster, 1995), was a national bestseller. He teaches writing at LSU in Baton Rouge, Louisiana, and edits *Exquisite Corpse: a Journal of Letters & Life*. He lives in New Orleans.